Gaining Ground

New Approaches to Poverty and Dependency

Charles Murray • Robert Royal
Glenn C. Loury • Michael Novak
Peter L. Berger

Foreword by Leslie Lenkowsky
Edited by Michael Cromartie

D1570263

Ethics and Public Policy Center • *Washington, D.C.*

Contents

Preface

ONE HUNDRED AND FIFTY YEARS ago in his "Memoir on Pauperism" Alexis de Tocqueville wrote: "I am deeply convinced that any permanent, regular, administrative system whose aim will be to provide for the needs of the poor, will breed more miseries than it can cure" and "will deprave the population that it wants to help and comfort." In modern industrialized societies, this statement may need some qualification, but recent analyses of our social welfare system suggest that de Tocqueville's fears were to a great extent justified.

Conservatives and liberals have been arguing for years about social programs designed to eliminate poverty and hunger in the United States. Often debates on social policy have degenerated into emotional claims about who is compassionate and who is not. There are signs that indicate our government not only has failed to win its War on Poverty but has actually made life worse for the poor themselves. Haunting problems have arisen that demand solutions: soaring illegitimacy rates, decline in the quality of education, growing crime, and increasing family deterioration. All of this has occurred despite huge outpourings of aid to welfare and poverty programs.

The interrelations of poverty, unemployment, transfer payments, and our moral responsibilities toward the "welfare underclass" will long occupy U.S. domestic policy debates. Each of the essays here draws upon our twenty years of experience with social programs and points toward new approaches to make them more responsive to reality.

The foreword to this collection is by Leslie Lenkowsky, a resident fellow at the American Enterprise Institute in Washington, D.C. Mr. Lenkowsky directs, with Michael Novak, a "social invention project" at AEI, aimed at rethinking social welfare policy.

Innovative approaches that seek to help the poor without creating dependency should win support from all points of the political spectrum. We can look forward to some surprising alliances between former adversaries. The

Ethics and Public Policy Center publishes these essays with the hope that they will stimulate new and effective social welfare policies.

Related studies published by the Center are *Crime and American Culture* by James Q. Wilson, *Patterns of Black Excellence* by Thomas Sowell, and *Ethnic Groups in History Textbooks* by Nathan Glazer and Reed Ueda.

In all Center publications the views expressed are those of the authors.

MICHAEL CROMARTIE, *Research Associate*
Ethics and Public Policy Center

Washington, D.C.
August 1985

Foreword

PUBLIC DEBATE ON POVERTY in America has entered a new phase. The old liberal welfare programs, useful as they were in some cases, have proved severely limited as a means for dealing with many social problems. Conservative policies, especially the reliance on an expanding economy to improve the lot of all, have also demonstrated their limits: too many poor people fall outside the economy for growth to help them significantly. Anyone who wants to help the poor today, therefore, must begin to think about new approaches to some old questions, particularly the question of how needy people may attain a measure of human dignity while avoiding debilitating dependency.

The essays collected here begin to do just that, though so much work must still be done to recast our social policies that these writers are for the most part offering preliminary ideas. Charles Murray is probably the best known of the new social analysts and the one with the most far-reaching vision of how a new American social policy might look. His book *Losing Ground: American Social Policy 1950–1980* deserves careful study not only for its thoroughness but also for its sincere concern that we stop inadvertently harming the very people we are trying to help.

Murray's analysis and recommendations have met with much impassioned criticism. Robert Royal's essay on these critiques attempts to clarify how partisan reactions have led to misunderstanding. Though Royal does not find Murray's argument a final answer to our current predicament, he concludes that the negative effects of liberal welfare policies should no longer be accepted as inevitable by-products of our good intentions.

Glenn C. Loury, Michael Novak, and Peter L. Berger each propose novel alternatives to our current social programs. Professor Loury examines the prospects for self-help in the black community. He argues that racial discrimination may ultimately be at *fault* for many difficulties faced by black Americans, but blacks themselves must now accept *responsibility* for their own futures if they are to become truly independent. As the number of households headed by single black females and black illegitimacy rates have mushroomed, says Loury, we have become aware that traditional welfare programs not only have failed to help, but also may have significantly harmed black family life. As a result, many Americans see little value in expanding welfare programs. Loury suggests that the black middle class must try to form links with the black poor. Those blacks who have already succeeded to some extent in American society in spite of poverty and racism can best counsel the poor on how to do the same. Some successful blacks may well be in a position to provide avenues out of the dead end of poverty.

Writing as a Catholic theologian in his essay, Michael Novak explains that the family is a central component of Catholic social teaching. Broken families are more likely to be poor than families with both parents present, says Novak, and a humane social policy will seek to support families and minimize family breakdowns. The family, in Novak's view, is the best institution we have for forming responsible, educated adults with a good chance at success in the American system.

Peter L. Berger argues that not only the family but all other mediating structures—those institutions that stand between the individual and the state, such as organized religion and community organizations—are essential to the vitality of a modern society. Government should respect these institutions and not seek to usurp their roles, says Berger. Local associations have a much more intimate contact with the persons who are in need. Hence their responses are likely to be more appropriate and better administered than federal programs with standards that must be applicable everywhere in the nation.

This year marks the fiftieth anniversary of the signing of the Social Security Act, the New Deal legislation that ushered in the American version of the "welfare state." It is altogether fitting that we use this occasion to examine our experience with programs aimed at helping the poor and other needy groups. To be effective, social policy must adapt to deal with new social problems or altered conditions. An honest review of the evidence suggests an increasing need for such changes today. Whether a welfare philosophy as popular and lasting as that of the Social Security Act can be found is uncertain, but the search is one which liberals and conservatives alike should undertake.

I commend the Ethics and Public Policy Center for making these essays more widely available and for its ambitious plans for a two-year program to explore new approaches to poverty. These should prove to be a vital addition to work in progress elsewhere.

LESLIE LENKOWSKY

What Do We Want?

CHARLES MURRAY

THE LEGITIMACY OF altering social institutions to achieve greater equality of material conditions is, though often assumed, rarely *argued* for," Robert Nozick observes, and so it has been in debate on social policy. Why pay for welfare? Why pay for Food Stamps? Why pay for scholarships for poor students? Most answers are not so much reasons as affirmations of faith. By and large, we have not for some years asked primitive questions about social policy. The debate over the size of the Food Stamps budget is vigorous. The debate over whether it is *right* that there be a Food Stamps budget has been limited to a few libertarians who are adequately answered, it is assumed, by the self-evident goodness of providing food to needy people.

I do not propose to argue the "why" questions in all their philosophical ramifications. Nor is this the place to try to construct a theory through which all competing answers may be reconciled. Rather, let us establish only that the answers to the "why" questions are not usually so abstract as "because it is the humane thing to do" or "because I am my brother's keeper." We are occasionally forced to fall back on these final and not very enlightening justifications, but usually we have something quite different in mind.

"Why Give Anything at All?"

If social policy may be construed, as I suggested at the beginning of the book, as transfers from the haves to the have-nots, the proper first question is, "What is the justification for any transfers at all?" Why should one person give *anything* to a stranger whose only claim to his help is a common citizenship?

Charles Murray is senior research fellow at the Manhattan Institute for Policy Research and the author of several books. This essay is adapted from chapters 15 and 17 of *Losing Ground: American Social Policy 1950–1980* (copyright © 1984 by Charles Murray) and is reprinted with permission of Basic Books, New York.

Suppose that I am not opposed to the notion of government transfers, but neither do I think that equality of outcome is always a good in itself. I attach considerable value to the principle that people get what they deserve. In other words, "I" am a fairly typical citizen with a middle-of-the-road, pragmatic political philosophy.

I am asked to consider the case of a man who has worked steadily for many years and, in his fifties, is thrown out of his job because the factory closes. Why should I transfer money to him—provide him with unemployment checks and, perhaps, permanent welfare support? The answer is not difficult. I may rationalize it any number of ways, but at bottom I consent to transfer money to him because I want to. The worker has plugged along as best he could, contributed his bit to the community, and now faces personal disaster. He is one of my fellows in a very meaningful way—"There but for the grace of God . . ."—and I am happy to see a portion of my income used to help him out. (I would not be happy to see so much of my income transferred that I am unable to meet my obligations to myself and my family, however.)

A second man, healthy and in the prime of life, refuses to work. I offer him a job, and he still refuses to work. I am called upon to answer the question again: Why should I transfer money to him? Why should I not let him starve, considering it a form of suicide?

It is a question to ponder without escape hatches. I may not assume that the man can be made to change his ways with the right therapeutic intervention. I may not assume that he has some mental or environmental handicap that relieves him of responsibility. He is a man of ordinary capacities who wishes to live off my work rather than work for himself. Why should I consent?

Suppose that I decide not to let him starve in the streets, for reasons having to do with the sanctity of life (I would prevent a suicide as well). The decision does not take me very far in setting up an ideal policy. At once, I run into choices when I compare his situation (we will call him the drone) with that of the laid-off worker.

Suppose that I have only enough resources either (a) to keep both alive at a bare subsistence level or (b) to support the laid-off worker at a decent standard of living and the drone at a near-starvation level. What would be the just policy? Would it be right, would it be fair, to make the worker live more miserably so that I might be more generous to the drone?

We may put the question more provocatively: Suppose that scarce resources were not a problem—that we could afford to support both at a decent standard of living. Should we do so? Is it morally appropriate to give the same level of support to the two men? Would it be right to offer the same respect to the two men? The same discretionary choice in how to use the help that was provided?

These are not rhetorical questions, nor are they questions about expedient policy. They ask about the justice and humanity of the alternatives. I submit that it is not humane to the laid-off worker to treat him the same as the drone. It is not just to accord the drone the respect that the laid-off worker has earned.

The point is that, in principle, most of us provide some kinds of assistance gladly, for intuitively obvious reasons. We provide other kinds of assistance for reasons that, when it comes down to it, are extremely hard to defend on either moral or practical grounds. An ethically ideal social policy—an *intuitively* satisfying one—would discriminate among recipients. It would attach a pat on the back to some transfers and give others begrudgingly.

We have yet to tackle the question of whether the point has anything to do with recipients in the workaday world. Who is to say that the drone has no justification for refusing to work (he was trained as a cook and we offer him a job sweeping floors)? Who is to say whether the laid-off worker is blameless for the loss of his job (his sloppy workmanship contributed to the factory's loss of business to the Japanese)? Who is to say that the income of the taxpaying donor is commensurate with his value to society—that he "deserves" his income any more than the drone deserves the gift of a part of it? But such questions define the operational barriers to establishing a social policy that discriminates among recipients according to their deserts. They do not touch on the legitimacy of the principle.

Transfers From Poor to Poor

When we think of transfers, we usually think in terms of economic transfers from richer to poorer. In reality, social policy can obligate one citizen to turn over a variety of "goods" as a donation on behalf of some other person; access to parking spaces reserved for the handicapped is a simple example.

Sometimes these noneconomic transfers, like the economic ones, are arranged so that the better-off give up something to the worse-off, and the argument about whether the transfer is appropriate follows the lines of the issues I have just raised. But in a surprising number of instances the transfers are mandated by the better-off, while the price must be paid by donors who are just as poor as the recipient.

Now suppose that the same hypothetical "I" considers the case of two students in an inner-city high school. Both come from poor families. Both have suffered equal deprivations and social injustices. They have the same intelligence and human potential. For whatever reasons—let us assume pure accident—the two students behave differently in school. One student (the good student) studies hard and pays attention in class. The other student (the mischievous student) does not study and instead creates disturbances, albeit good-natured disturbances, in the classroom.

I observe a situation in which the teacher expels the mischievous student from the classroom more or less at will. The result is that he becomes further alienated from school, drops out, and eventually ends up on welfare or worse. I know that the cause of this sequence of events (his behavior in class) was no worse than the behavior of millions of middle-class students who suffer nothing like the same penalty. They too are kicked out of class when they act up, but for a variety of reasons they stay in school and eventually do well. Further yet, I know that the behavior of the teacher toward the student is biased and unfairly harsh because the student is an inner-city black and the teacher is a suburban white who neither understands nor sympathizes with such students.

On all counts, then, I observe that the mischievous student expelled from the classroom is a victim who deserves a system that does not unfairly penalize him. I therefore protect him against the bias and arbitrariness of the teacher. The teacher cannot expel the student from class unless the student's behavior meets certain criteria far beyond the ordinary talking and laughing out of turn that used to get him in trouble.

The result, let us say, is that the student continues to act as before, but remains in the classroom. Other students also respond to the reality of the greater latitude they now have. The amount of teaching is reduced, and so is the ability of students to concentrate on their work even if they want to.

I know, however, that some benefits are obtained. The mischievous student who formerly dropped out of school does not. He obtains his diploma, and with it some advantages in the form of greater education (he learned something, although not much, while he stayed in school) and a credential to use when applying for a job.

This benefit has been obtained at a price. The price is not money—let us say it costs no more to run the school under the new policy than under the old. No transfers have been exacted from the white middle class. The transfer instead is wholly from the good student to the mischievous one. For I find that the quality of education obtained by the good student deteriorated badly, both because the teacher had less time and energy for teaching and because the classroom environment was no longer suitable for studying. One poor and disadvantaged student has been compelled (he had no choice in the matter) to give up part of his education so that the other student could stay in the classroom.

What is my rationale for enforcing this transfer? In what sense did the good student have an excess of educational opportunity that he could legitimately be asked to sacrifice?

The example has deliberately been constructed so that neither student was intrinsically more deserving than the other. The only difference between the two was behavioral, with one student behaving in a more desirable way than the other student. Even under these unrealistically neutral conditions, it is hard to avoid the conclusion that the transfer was unjustifiable. Now, let us make the example more realistic.

A student who reaches adolescence in an inner-city school with high motivation to study and learn does not do so by accident. The motivation is likely to reflect merit — on the student's part, on the parents' part, or on a combination of the two. In the good student's behavior I am observing not just a "desirable" response but a praiseworthy one.

Further, if we make the example realistic, the good student does not transfer simply an abstract deterioration in the quality of education, from a potentially fine education to a merely adequate one. The more likely loss is a much greater one, from an adequate education that might have prepared the good student to take advantage of opportunities for higher education to an inadequate education that leaves the good student, no matter how well motivated, without essential tools to pursue basic routes to advancement.

Once again, let me consider my rationale without giving myself an easy out. I may not assume that classroom instruction is not really affected by disruption; it is. I may not assume that counselors will be able shortly to change the behavior of the mischievous student. I may not assume that the school will provide separate tracks for the attentive student; the same philosophy that led to greater student rights also led to restrictions and even prohibitions on separate tracks for the better students. Most of all, I may not assume that the good student is superhuman. He may be admirable, but he is not necessarily able to get himself a good education no matter what obstacles I put in his way.

Such transfers from poor to poor are at the heart of the inequities of social policy. Saying that we meant well does not quite cover our transgressions. Even during the period of the most active reform we could not help being aware, if only at the back of our minds, of certain moral problems. When poor delinquents arrested for felonies were left on probation, as the elite wisdom prescribed they should be, the persons put most at risk were poor people who lived in their neighborhoods. They, not the elite, gave up the greater part of the good called "safety" so that the disadvantaged delinquent youth should not experience the injustice of punishment. When job-training programs were set up to function at the level of the least competent, it was the most competent trainees who had to sacrifice their opportunities to reach their potentials. When social policy reinforced the ethic that certain jobs are too demeaning to ask people to do, it was those who preferred such jobs to welfare whose basis for self-respect was stripped from them.

More generally, social policy after the mid-1960s demanded an extraordinary range of transfers from the most capable poor to the least capable, from the most law-abiding to the least law-abiding, and from the most responsible to the least responsible. In return, we gave little to these most deserving persons except easier access to welfare for themselves—the one thing they found hardest to put to "good use."

We blinked at these realities at the time. The homogenizing process helped us to blink; the poor were all poor, all more or less in the same situation, we said. All *would* be deserving, we preferred to assume, if they had not been so exploited by society, by the system. But at bottom it is difficult to imagine under what logic we thought these transfers appropriate.

The Net Happiness Challenge

The peculiarity of a transfer, as opposed to the other uses of tax monies, is that the direct benefit goes only to the recipient. If I pay for garbage collection, I, the payer, get a benefit. My garbage disappears. I may argue about whether the garbage collection service is efficiently operated and whether I am getting value for money, but I do not argue about whether, somehow, my garbage must be made to disappear, and so must my neighbor's garbage. If I pay for Food Stamps with my tax dollars, the government is making quite a different request of me and undertaking a much different responsibility. The government judges that my income is large enough that a portion of it should be given to someone whose income, the government has decided, is too small. And when, for example, the Food Stamps are buying milk for a malnourished child, I am pleased that they should do so. But I may legitimately ask two things of the government that exercises such authority. First, I may ask that the government be *right* — right in deciding that, in some cosmic scheme of things, my resources are "large enough" and the recipient's are "too small." Second, I may ask that the transfer be successful, and therein lies a problem.

If the transfer is successful, I, the donor, can be satisfied on either of two grounds: general humanitarianism ("I am doing good") or more self-interested calculations that make transfers not so very different from police service or garbage collection. For the sake of my own quality of life, I do not want to live in a Calcutta with people sleeping in the streets in front of my house. If it is true that putting delinquents in jail only makes them into worse criminals later on, then putting the neighbors at just a little more risk by leaving delinquents at large is worth it *to them*, because eventually it will reduce their risk. The short-term injustices are rescued by a long-term greater good for everyone.

Whether I choose humanitarianism or long-term self-interest as the basis for approving the transfer, I must confront the "net happiness" challenge. If the first questions of social policy ask why we approve of transfers at all, the next questions ask how we know whether our expectations are being justified. How, in an ideal world, would we measure "success" in assessing a transfer?

The social scientists who measure the effects of transfers look for success at two levels and of necessity ignore a third. The first level is, "Did the transfer reach the people it was intended to reach in the intended form?" (Do Food Stamps reach people who need extra food money?) The second level is, "Did the transfer have the intended direct effect on the behavior or condition of the recipients?" (Do Food Stamps improve nutrition?) The third, unattainable level is, "Did the transfer, in the long run, add to net happiness in the world?"

We may presume that better housing, nutrition, and medical care contribute to less misery and more happiness; so also do good parents, a loving spouse, safe streets, personal freedom, and the respect of one's neighbors. We know how to measure some of these aspects of the quality of life; others we cannot measure at all; and, most certainly, we are unable to compare their relative worth or to add up a net total. We have no "misery" or "happiness" indexes worthy of the name. But the concept of reducing misery and increasing happiness is indispensable to deciding whether a social policy is working or failing.

With that in mind, let us consider yet another hypothetical example. In this case, I am deciding upon my stance in support or opposition of a policy that automatically provides an adequate living allowance for all single women with children. I am informed that one consequence of this policy is that large numbers of the children get better nutrition and medical care than they would otherwise obtain. Based on this known fact and no others, I support the program.

Now, let us assume two more known facts, that the program induces births by women who otherwise would have had fewer children (or had them under different circumstances), and that child abuse and neglect among these children runs at twice the national average. Does this alter my judgment about whether the allowance is a net good—that it is better to have it than not have it? I must now balance the better health of some children against the pain suffered by others who would not have suffered the pain if the program had not existed. I decide—although I wish I could avoid the question altogether—that, all in all, I still support the program.

What if the incidence of abuse and neglect is three times as high? Five times? Ten times? A hundred times?

The crossover point will be different for different people. But a crossover will occur. At some point, I will say that the benefits of better nutrition and medical care are outweighed by the suffering of the abused and neglected children. What then is the humane policy? Once more I must avoid false escape hatches. I may continue to search for a strategy that does not have the overbalancing side-effects. But what is my position toward the existing program in the meantime?

All of these examples—the worker versus the drone, the good student versus the bad student, the children helped versus the children hurt—are intended to emphasize a reality we tend to skirt. Devising a system of transfers that is just, fair, and compassionate involves extraordinarily difficult moral choices in which the issue is not how much good we can afford to do (as the choice is usually put), but how to do good at all. In the debate over social policy, the angels are not arrayed against the accountants.

The examples do not force one set of principles over all others. A socialist may use them in support of an internally consistent rationale for sweeping redistributive measures. At the other end of the spectrum, a libertarian may use them to support the eradication of transfers altogether. For those who fall somewhere in the middle, two more modest conclusions about what constitutes a just and humane social policy are warranted.

The first conclusion is that transfers are inherently treacherous. They can be useful; they can be needed; they can be justified. But we should approach them as a good physician uses a dangerous drug — not at all if possible, and no more than absolutely necessary otherwise.

The second conclusion is that, as a general rule, compulsory transfers from one poor person to another are uncomfortably like robbery. When we require money transfers from the obviously rich to the obviously poor, we at least have some room for error. Mistaken policies may offend our sense of right and wrong, but no great harm has been done to the donor. The same is not true of the noneconomic transfers from poor to poor. We have no margin for error at all. If we are even a little bit wrong about the consequences of the transfer, we are likely to do great injustices to people who least deserve to bear the burden.

And that, finally, is what makes the question of social policy not one of polite philosophical dispute but one of urgent importance. For the examples in this chapter are not really hypothetical. They are drawn directly from the data we reviewed. It is impossible to examine the statistics on a topic such as single teenage mothers without admitting that we are witnessing a tragedy. *If* it had been inevitable, *if* there had been nothing we could have done to avoid it, then we could retain the same policies, trying to do more of the same and hoping for improvement. But once we must entertain the possibility that we are bringing it on ourselves, as I am arguing that both logic and evidence compel us to do, then it is time to reconsider a social policy that salves our consciences ("Look how compassionate I am") at the expense of those whom we wished to help.

A Proposal for Social Policy and Race

Real reform of American social policy is out of the question until we settle the race issue. We have been dancing around it since 1964, wishing it would go away and at the same time letting it dominate, *sub rosa*, the formation of social policy.

The source of our difficulties has been the collision, with enormous attendant national anxiety and indecision, of two principles so much a part of the American ethos that hardly anyone, whatever his political position, can wholly embrace one and reject the other. The principles are equal treatment and a fair shake.

The principle of equal treatment demands that we all play by the same rules—which would seem to rule out any policy that gives preferential treatment to anyone. A fair shake demands that everyone have a reasonably equal chance at the brass ring—or at least a reasonably equal chance to get on the merry-go-round.

Thus hardly anyone, no matter how strictly noninterventionist, can watch with complete equanimity when a black child is deprived of a chance to develop his full potential for reasons that may be directly traced to a heritage of exploitation by whites. Neither can anyone, no matter how devoted to Affirmative Action, watch with complete equanimity when a white job applicant is turned down for a job in favor of a black who is less qualified. Something about it is fundamentally unfair—un-American—no matter how admirable the ultimate goal.

Until 1965, the principles of equal treatment and a fair shake did not compete. They created no tension. Their application to racial policy was simple: Make the nation color-blind. People were to be judged on their merits. But then the elite wisdom changed. Blacks were to be helped to catch up.

I spent many chapters tracing the results. In summarizing these results as they pertain to the poorest blacks, this harsh judgment is warranted: If an impartial observer from another country were shown the data on the black lower class from 1950 to 1980 but given no information about contemporaneous changes in society or public policy, that observer would infer that racial discrimination against the black poor increased drastically during the late 1960s and 1970s. No explanation except a surge in outright, virulent discrimination would as easily explain to a "blind" observer why things went so wrong.

New Forms of Racism

Such an explanation is for practical purposes correct. Beginning in the last half of the 1960s, the black poor were subjected to new forms of racism with effects that outweighed the waning of the old forms of racism. Before the 1960s, we had a black underclass that was held down because blacks were systematically treated differently from whites, by whites. Now, we have a black underclass that is held down for the same generic reason—because blacks are systematically treated differently from whites, by whites.

The problem consists of a change in the nature of white condescension toward blacks. Historically, virtually all whites condescended toward virtually all blacks; there is nothing new in that. The condescension could be vicious in intent, in the form of "keeping niggers in their place." It could be benign, as in the excessive solicitousness with which whites who considered themselves enlightened tended to treat blacks.

These forms of condescension came under withering attack during the civil rights movement, to such an extent that certain manifestations of the condescension disappeared altogether in some circles. A variety of factors— among them, simply greater representation of blacks in the white professional world of work—made it easier for whites to develop relationships of authentic equality and respect with black colleagues. But from a policy standpoint, it became clear only shortly after the War on Poverty began that henceforth the black lower class was to be the object of a new condescension that would become intertwined with every aspect of social policy. Race is central to the problem of reforming social policy, not because it is intrinsically so but because the debate about what to do has been perverted by the underlying consciousness among whites that "they"—the people to be helped by social policy—are predominantly black, and blacks are owed a debt.

The result was that the intelligentsia and the policymakers, coincident with the revolution in social policy, began treating the black poor in ways that they would never consider treating people they respected. Is the black crime rate skyrocketing? Look at the black criminal's many grievances against society. Are black illegitimate birth rates five times those of whites? We must remember that blacks have a much broader view of the family than we do— aunts and grandmothers fill in. Did black labor-force participation among the young plummet? We can hardly blame someone for having too much pride to work at a job sweeping floors. Are black high-school graduates illiterate? The educational system is insensitive. Are their test scores a hundred points lower than others? The tests are biased. Do black youngsters lose jobs to white youngsters because their mannerisms and language make them incomprehensible to their prospective employers? The culture of the ghetto has its own validity.

That the condescension should be so deep and pervasive is monumentally ironic, for the injunction to respect the poor (after all, they are not to blame) was hammered home in the tracts of the Office of Economic Opportunity and radical intellectuals. But condescension is the correct descriptor. Whites began to tolerate and make excuses for behavior among blacks that whites would disdain in themselves or their children.

The expression of this attitude in policy has been a few obvious steps — Affirmative Action, minority set-asides in government contracts, and the like — but the real effect was the one that I discussed in the history of the period. The white elite could not at one time cope with two reactions. They could not simultaneously feel compelled to make restitution for past wrongs to blacks and blame blacks for not taking advantage of their new opportunities. The system *had* to be blamed, and any deficiencies demonstrated by blacks had to be overlooked or covered up — by whites.

A central theme of this book has been that the consequences were disastrous for poor people of all races, but for poor blacks especially, and most emphatically for poor blacks in all-black communities — precisely that population that was the object of the most unremitting sympathy.

My proposal for dealing with the racial issue in social welfare is to repeal every bit of legislation and reverse every court decision that in any way requires, recommends, or awards differential treatment according to race, and thereby put us back onto the track that we left in 1965. We may argue about the appropriate limits of government intervention in trying to enforce the ideal, but at least it should be possible to identify the ideal: Race is not a morally admissible reason for treating one person differently from another. Period.

A Proposal for Education

There is no such thing as an undeserving five-year-old. Society, in the form of government intervention, is quite limited in what it can do to make up for many of the deficiencies of life that an unlucky five-year-old experiences; it can, however, provide a good education and thereby give the child a chance at a different future.

The objective is a system that provides more effective education of the poor and disadvantaged. The objective is also to construct what is, in my view, a just system — one that does not sacrifice one student's interests to another's, and one that removes barriers in the way of those who want most badly to succeed and are prepared to make the greatest effort to do so. So once again let us put ourselves in the position of bureaucrats of sweeping authority and large budgets. How shall we make things better?

We begin by installing a completely free educational system that goes from preschool to the loftiest graduate degrees, removing economic barriers entirely. Having done so, however, we find little change from the system that prevailed in 1980. Even then, kindergarten through high school were free to the student, and federal grants and loans worth $4.4 billion *plus* a very extensive system of private scholarships and loans were available for needy students who wanted to continue their education. By making the system entirely free, we are not making more education newly accessible to large numbers of people, nor have we done anything about the quality of education.

We then make a second and much more powerful change. For many years, the notion of a voucher system for education has enjoyed a periodic vogue. In its pure form, it would give each parent of a child of school age a voucher that the parent could use to pay for schooling at any institution to which the child could gain admittance. The school would redeem the voucher for cash from the government. The proposals for voucher systems have generally foundered on accusations that they are a tool for the middle class and would leave the disadvantaged in the lurch. My proposition is rather different: A voucher system is the single most powerful method available to us to improve the education of the poor and disadvantaged. Vouchers thus become the second component of our educational reforms.

For one large segment of the population of poor and disadvantaged, the results are immediate, unequivocal, and dramatic. I refer to children whose parents take an active role in overseeing and encouraging their children's education. Such parents have been fighting one of the saddest of the battles of the poor—doing everything they can within the home environment, only to see their influence systematically undermined as soon as their children get out the door. When we give such parents vouchers, we find that they behave very much as their affluent counterparts behave when they are deciding upon a private school. They visit prospective schools, interview teachers, and place their children in schools that are demanding of the students and accountable to the parents for results. I suggest that when we give such parents vouchers, we will observe substantial convergence of black and white test scores in a single generation. All that such parents have ever needed is an educational system that operates on the same principles they do.

This is a sufficient improvement to justify the system, for we are in a no-lose situation with regard to the children whose parents do not play their part effectively. These children are sent to bad schools or no schools at all—just as they were in the past. How much worse can it be under the new system?

This defect in the voucher system leaves us, however, with a substantial number of students who are still getting no education through no fault of their own. Nor can we count on getting results if we round them up and dispatch them willy-nilly to the nearest accredited school. A school that can motivate and teach a child when there is backup from home cannot necessarily teach the children we are now discussing. Many of them are poor not only in money. Many have been developmentally impoverished as well, receiving very little of the early verbal and conceptual stimulation that happens as a matter of course when parents expect their children to be smart. Some arrive at the school door already believing themselves to be stupid, expecting to fail. We can be as angry as we wish at their parents, but we are still left with the job of devising a school that works for these children. What do we do — not in terms of a particular pedagogical program or curriculum, but in broad strokes?

First, whatever else, we decide to create a world that makes sense in the context of the society we want them to succeed in. The school is not an extension of the neighborhood. Within the confines of the school building and school day, we create a world that may seem as strange and irrelevant as Oz.

We do not do so with uniforms or elaborate rules or inspirational readings — the embellishments are left up to the school. Rather, we install one simple, inflexible procedure. Each course has an entrance test. Tenth-grade geometry has an entrance test; so does first-grade reading. Entrance tests for simple courses are simple; entrance tests for hard courses are hard. Their purpose is not to identify the best students, but to make sure that any student who gets in can, with an honest effort, complete the course work.

Our system does not carry with it any special teaching technique. It does, however, give the teacher full discretion over enforcing an orderly working environment. The teacher's only obligation is to teach those who want to learn.

The system is also infinitely forgiving. A student who has just flunked algebra three times running can enroll in that or any other math class for which he can pass the entrance test. He can enroll even if he has just been kicked out of three other classes for misbehavior. The question is never "What have you been in the past?" but always "What are you being as of now?"

The evolving outcomes of the system are complex. Some students begin by picking the easiest, least taxing courses, and approach them with as little motivation as their counterparts under the current system. Perhaps among this set of students are some who cannot or will not complete even the simplest courses. They drop by the wayside, failures of the system.

Among those who do complete courses, *any* courses, five things happen, all of them positive. First, the system is so constructed that to get into a course is in itself a small success ("I passed!"). Second, the students go into the course with a legitimate reason for believing that they can do the work; they passed a valid test that says they can. Third, they experience a success when they complete the course. Fourth, they experience—directly—a cause-effect relationship between their success in one course and their ability to get into the next course, no matter how small a step upward that next course may be. Fifth, all the while this is going on, they are likely to be observing other students *no different from them*—no richer, no smarter—who are moving upward faster than they are but using the same mechanism.

What of those who are disappointed, who try to get into a class and fail? Some will withdraw into themselves and be forever fearful of taking a chance on failure—as almost all do under the current system anyway. But there is a gradation to risk, and a peculiar sort of guarantee of success in our zero-transfer system. Whatever class a student finally takes, the student will have succeeded in gaining entrance to it. He will go into the classroom with official certification—based on reality—that he will be able to learn the material if he gives it an honest effort. The success-failure, cause-effect features of the system are indispensable for teaching some critical lessons:

- Effort is often rewarded with success.
- Effort is not *always* rewarded with success.
- Failure in one instance does not mean inability to succeed in anything else.
- Failure in one try does not mean perpetual failure.
- The better the preparation, the more likely the success.

None of these lessons is taught as well or as directly under the system prevailing in our current education of the disadvantaged. The central failing of the educational system for the poor and disadvantaged, and most especially poor and disadvantaged blacks, is not that it fails to provide meaningful ways for a student to succeed, though that is part of it. The central failing is not that ersatz success—fake curricula, fake grades, fake diplomas—sets the students up for failure when they leave the school, though that too is part of it. The central failing is that the system does not teach disadvantaged students, who see permanent failure all around them, *how to fail.*

For students who are growing up expecting (whatever their dreams may be) ultimately to be a failure, with failure writ large, the first essential contravening lesson is that failure can come in small, digestible packages. Failure can be dealt with. It can be absorbed, analyzed, and converted to an asset.

We are now discussing a population of students—the children of what has become known as "the underclass"—that comes to the classroom with an array of disadvantages beyond simple economic poverty. I am not suggesting that, under our hypothetical system, all children of the underclass will become motivated students forthwith. Rather, some will. Perhaps it will be a small proportion; perhaps a large one. Certainly the effect interacts with the inherent abilities of the children involved. But some effect will be observed. Some children who are at the very bottom of the pile in the disadvantages they bear will act on the change in the reality of their environment. It will be an improvement over the situation in the system we have replaced, in which virtually none of them gets an education in anything except the futility of hoping.

A Proposal for Public Welfare

I begin with the proposition that it is within our resources to do enormous good for some people quickly. We have available to us a program that would convert a large proportion of the younger generation of hardcore unemployed into steady workers making a living wage. The same program would drastically reduce births to single teenage girls. It would reverse the trendline in the breakup of poor families. It would measurably increase the upward socioeconomic mobility of poor families. These improvements would affect some millions of persons.

All these are results that have eluded the efforts of the social programs installed since 1965, yet, from everything we know, there is no real question about whether they would occur under the program I propose. A wide variety of persuasive evidence from our own culture and around the world, from experimental data and longitudinal studies, from theory and practice, suggests that the program would achieve such results.

The proposed program, our final and most ambitious thought experiment, consists of scrapping the entire federal welfare and income-support structure for working-age persons, including AFDC (Aid to Families with Dependent Children), Medicaid, Food Stamps, Unemployment Insurance, Worker's Compensation, subsidized housing, disability insurance, and the rest. It would leave the working-age person with no recourse whatever except the job market, family members, friends, and public or private locally funded services. It is the Alexandrian solution: cut the knot, for there is no way to untie it.

It is difficult to examine such a proposal dispassionately. Those who dislike paying for welfare are for it without thinking. Others reflexively imagine bread lines and people starving in the streets. But as a means of gaining fresh perspective on the problem of effective reform, let us consider what this hypothetical society might look like.

A large majority of the population is unaffected. A surprising number of the huge American middle and working classes go from birth to grave without using any social welfare benefits until they receive their first Social Security check. Another portion of the population is technically affected, but the change in income is so small or so sporadic that it makes no difference in quality of life. A third group comprises persons who have to make new arrangements and behave in different ways. Sons and daughters who fail to find work continue to live with their parents or relatives or friends. Teenage mothers have to rely on support from their parents or the father of the child and perhaps work as well. People laid off from work have to use their own savings or borrow from others to make do until the next job is found. All these changes involve great disruption in expectations and accustomed roles.

Along with the disruptions go other changes in behavior. Some parents do not want their young adult children continuing to live off their income, and become quite insistent about their children learning skills and getting jobs. This attitude is most prevalent among single mothers who have to depend most critically on the earning power of their offspring.

Parents tend to become upset at the prospect of a daughter's bringing home a baby that must be entirely supported on an already inadequate income. Some become so upset that they spend considerable parental energy avoiding such an eventuality. Potential fathers of such babies find themselves under more pressure not to cause such a problem, or to help with its solution if it occurs.

Adolescents who were not job-ready find they are job-ready after all. It turns out that they can work for low wages and accept the discipline of the workplace if the alternative is grim enough. After a few years, many—not all, but many—find that they have acquired salable skills, or that they are at the right place at the right time, or otherwise find that the original entry-level job has gradually been transformed into a secure job paying a decent wage. A few—not a lot, but a few—find that the process leads to affluence.

Perhaps the most rightful, deserved benefit goes to the much larger population of low-income families who have been doing things right all along and have been punished for it: the young man who has taken responsibility for his wife and child even though his friends with the same choice have called him a fool; the single mother who has worked full time and forfeited her right to welfare for very little extra money; the parents who have set an example for their children even as the rules of the game have taught their children that the example is outmoded. For these millions of people, the instantaneous result is that no one makes fun of them any longer. The longer-term result will be that they regain the status that is properly theirs. They will not only be the bedrock upon which the community is founded (which they always have been), they will be recognized as such. The process whereby they regain their position is not magical, but a matter of logic. When it becomes highly dysfunctional for a person to be dependent, status will accrue to being independent, and in fairly short order. Noneconomic rewards will once again reinforce the economic rewards of being a good parent and provider.

The prospective advantages are real and extremely plausible. In fact, if a government program of the traditional sort (one that would "do" something rather than simply get out of the way) could *as plausibly* promise these advantages, its passage would be a foregone conclusion. Congress, yearning for programs that are not retreads of failures, would be prepared to spend billions. Negative side-effects (as long as they were the traditionally acceptable negative side-effects) would be brushed aside as trivial in return for the benefits. For let me be quite clear: I am not suggesting that we dismantle income support for the working-aged to balance the budget or punish welfare cheats. I am hypothesizing, with the advantage of powerful collateral evidence, that the lives of large numbers of poor people would be radically changed for the better.

There is, however, a fourth segment of the population yet to be considered, those who are pauperized by the withdrawal of government supports and unable to make alternative arrangements: the teenage mother who has no one to turn to; the incapacitated or the inept who are thrown out of the house; those to whom economic conditions have brought long periods in which there is no work to be had; those with illnesses not covered by insurance. What of these situations?

The first resort is the network of local services. Poor communities in our hypothetical society are still dotted with storefront health clinics, emergency relief agencies, employment services, legal services. They depend for support on local taxes or local philanthropy, and the local taxpayers and philanthropists tend to scrutinze them rather closely. But, by the same token, they also receive considerably more resources than they formerly did. The dismantling of the federal services has poured tens of billions of dollars back into the private economy. Some of that money no doubt has been spent on Mercedes and summer homes on the Cape. But some has been spent on capital investments that generate new jobs. And some has been spent on increased local services to the poor, voluntarily or as decreed by the municipality. In many cities, the coverage provided by this network of agencies is more generous, more humane, more wisely distributed, and more effective in its results than the services formerly subsidized by the federal government.

But we must expect that a large number of people will fall between the cracks. How might we go about trying to retain the advantages of a zero-level welfare system and still address the residual needs?

As we think about the nature of the population still in need, it becomes apparent that their basic problem in the vast majority of the cases is the lack of a job, and this problem is temporary. What they need is something to tide them over while finding a new place in the economy. So our first step is to re-install the Unemployment Insurance program in more or less its previous form. Properly administered, unemployment insurance makes sense. Even if it is restored with all the defects of current practice, the negative effects of Unemployment Insurance *alone* are relatively minor. Our objective is not to wipe out chicanery or to construct a theoretically unblemished system, but to meet legitimate human needs without doing more harm than good. Unemployment Insurance is one of the least harmful ways of contributing to such ends. Thus the system has been amended to take care of the victims of short-term swings in the economy.

Who is left? We are now down to the hardest of the hard core of the welfare-dependent. They have no jobs. They have been unable to find jobs (or have not tried to find jobs) for a longer period of time than the unemployment benefits cover. They have no families who will help. They have no friends who will help. For some reason, they cannot get help from local services or private charities except for the soup kitchen and a bed in the Salvation Army hall.

What will be the size of this population? We have never tried a zero-level federal welfare system under conditions of late-twentieth-century national wealth, so we cannot do more than speculate. But we may speculate. Let us ask of whom the population might consist and how they might fare.

For any category of "needy" we may name, we find ourselves driven to one of two lines of thought. Either the person is in a category that is going to be at the top of the list of services that localities vote for themselves, and at the top of the list of private services, or the person is in a category where help really is not all that essential or desirable. The burden of the conclusion is not that every single person will be taken care of, but that the extent of resources to deal with needs is likely to be very great—not based on wishful thinking, but on extrapolations from reality.

To illustrate, let us consider the plight of the stereotypical welfare mother—never married, no skills, small children, no steady help from a man. It is safe to say that, now as in the 1950s, there is no one who has less sympathy from the white middle class, which is to be the source of most of the money for the private and local services we envision. Yet this same white middle class is a soft touch for people trying to make it on their own, and a soft touch for "deserving" needy mothers—AFDC was one of the most widely popular of the New Deal welfare measures, intended as it was for widows with small children. Thus we may envision two quite different scenarios.

In one scenario, the woman is presenting the local or private service with this proposition: "Help me find a job and day-care for my children, and I will take care of the rest." In effect, she puts herself into the same category as the widow and the deserted wife—identifies herself as one of the most obviously deserving of the deserving poor. Welfare mothers who want to get into the labor force are likely to find a wide range of help. In the other scenario, she asks for an outright and indefinite cash grant—in effect, a private or local version of AFDC—so that she can stay with the children and not hold a job. In the latter case, it is very easy to imagine situations in which she will not be able to find a local service or a private philanthropy to provide the help she seeks. The question we must now ask is: What's so bad about that? If children were always better off being with their mother all day and if, by the act of giving birth, a mother acquired the inalienable right to be with the child, then her situation would be unjust to her and injurious to her children. Neither assertion can be defended, however—especially not in the 1980s, when more mothers of all classes work away from the home than ever before, and even more especially not in view of the empirical record for the children growing up under the current welfare system. Why should the mother be exempted by the system from the pressures that must affect everyone else's decision to work?

As we survey these prospects, important questions remain unresolved. The first of these is why, if federal social transfers are treacherous, should locally mandated transfers be less so? Why should a municipality be permitted to legislate its own AFDC or Food Stamp program if their results are so inherently bad?

Part of the answer lies in conceptions of freedom. I have deliberately avoided raising them — the discussion is about how to help the disadvantaged, not about how to help the advantaged cut their taxes, to which arguments for personal freedom somehow always get diverted. Nonetheless, the point is valid: Local or even state systems leave much more room than a federal system for everyone, donors and recipients alike, to exercise freedom of choice about the kind of system they live under. Laws are more easily made and changed, and people who find them unacceptable have much more latitude in going somewhere more to their liking.

But the freedom of choice argument, while legitimate, is not necessary. We may put the advantages of local systems in terms of the Law of Imperfect Selection. A federal system must inherently employ very crude, inaccurate rules for deciding who gets what kind of help. At the opposite extreme — a neighbor helping a neighbor, a family member helping another family member — the law loses its validity nearly altogether. Very fine-grained judgments based on personal knowledge are being made about specific people and changing situations. In neighborhoods and small cities, the procedures can still bring much individualized information to bear on decisions. Even systems in large cities and states can do much better than a national system; a decaying industrial city in the Northeast and a booming sunbelt city of the same size can and probably should adopt much different rules about who gets what and how much.

A final and equally powerful argument for not impeding local systems is diversity. We know much more in the 1980s than we knew in the 1960s about what does not work. We have a lot to learn about what *does* work. Localities have been a rich source of experiments. Marva Collins in Chicago gives us an example of how a school can bring inner-city students up to national norms. Sister Falaka Fattah in Philadelphia shows us how homeless youths can be rescued from the streets. There are numberless such lessons waiting to be learned from the diversity of local efforts. By all means, let a hundred flowers bloom, and if the federal government can play a useful role in lending a hand and spreading the word of successes, so much the better.

The ultimate unresolved question about our proposal to abolish income maintenance for the working-aged is how many people will fall through the cracks. In whatever detail we try to foresee the consequences, the objection may always be raised: We cannot be *sure* that everyone will be taken care of in the degree to which we would wish. But this observation by no means settles the question. If one may point in objection to the child now fed by Food Stamps who would go hungry, one may also point with satisfaction to the child who would have an entirely different and better future. Hungry children should be fed; there is no argument about that. It is no less urgent that children be allowed to grow up in a system free of the forces that encourage them to remain poor and dependent. If a strategy reasonably promises to remove those forces, after so many attempts to "help the poor" have failed, it is worth thinking about.

But that rationale is too vague. Let me step outside the persona I have employed and put the issue in terms of one last intensely personal hypothetical example. Let us suppose that you, a parent, could know that tomorrow your own child would be made an orphan. You have a choice. You may put your child with an extremely poor family, so poor that your child will be badly clothed and will indeed sometimes be hungry. But you also know that the parents have worked hard all their lives, will make sure your child goes to school and studies, and will teach your child that independence is a primary value. Or you may put your child with a family with parents who have never worked, who will be incapable of overseeing your child's education — but who have plenty of food and good clothes, provided by others. If the choice about where one would put one's own child is as clear to you as it is to me, on what grounds does one justify support of a system that, indirectly but without doubt, makes the other choice for other children? The answer that "What we really want is a world where that choice is not forced upon us" is no answer. We have tried to have it that way. We failed. Everything we know about why we failed tells us that more of the same will not make the dilemma go away.

Escapism

It is entertaining to indulge in speculations about solutions, but they remain only speculations. Congress will not abolish income-maintenance for the working-aged. The public school system is not in jeopardy of replacement by vouchers. The federal government will not abandon legalized racial discrimination when it is thought to help the underdog. More generally, it is hard to imagine any significant reform of social policy in the near future. When one thinks of abolishing income maintenance, for example, one must recall that ours is a system that, faced with the bankruptcy of Social Security in the early 1980s, went into paroxysms of anxiety at the prospect of delaying the cost-of-living increase for six months.

But the cautiousness of the system is not in itself worrisome. Reforms should be undertaken carefully and slowly, and often not at all. What should worry us instead is a peculiar escapism that has gripped the consideration of social policy. It seems that those who legislate and administer and write about social policy can tolerate any increase in actual suffering as long as the system in place does not explicitly permit it. It is better, by the logic we have been living with, that we try to take care of 100 percent of the problem and make matters worse than that we solve 75 percent of the problem with a solution that does not try to do anything about the rest.

Escapism is a natural response. Most of us want to help. It makes us feel bad to think of neglected children and rat-infested slums, and we are happy to pay for the thought that people who are good at taking care of such things are out there. If the numbers of neglected children and numbers of rats seem to be going up instead of down, it is understandable that we choose to focus on how much we put into the effort instead of what comes out. The tax checks we write buy us, for relatively little money and no effort at all, a quieted conscience. The more we pay, the more certain we can be that we have done our part, and it is essential that we feel that way regardless of what we accomplish. A solution that would have us pay less *and* acknowledge that some would go unhelped is unacceptable.

To this extent, the barrier to radical reform of social policy is not the pain it would cause the intended beneficiaries of the present system, but the pain it would cause the donors. The real contest about the direction of social policy is not between people who want to cut budgets and people who want to help. When reforms finally do occur, they will happen not because stingy people have won, but because generous people have stopped kidding themselves.

Charles Murray and His Critics

ROBERT ROYAL

WHAT IS IT ABOUT Charles Murray's *Losing Ground: American Social Policy 1950–1980* (Basic Books, 1984) that has evoked such violent reactions? After initial shock at its publication last September, liberals have countered with a cataract of criticism. Socialist Michael Harrington denigrates Murray's use of statistics as "shoddy scholarship." Archbishop Rembert Weakland, chairman of the committee drafting the bishops' pastoral letter on the U.S. economy, dismisses Murray's social analysis as a "Malthusian" solution to the problem of poverty. Robert Kuttner, a contributing editor of the *New Republic* and author of a book that reaches conclusions opposed to Murray's, best captures the growing reaction in other quarters: "It's one of the few times liberals have successfully ganged up on a conservative. . . . Here is somebody who was set up real big and shot down real big. You don't get that every day. . . . Now it's 'Hold him so I can hit him again.' "

Charles Murray brings out the bully in normally tolerant and liberal magazine editors, as well as he might, since his ideas have virtually monopolized Washington domestic policy debates. *Washington Post* editorial page editor Meg Greenfield was moved to complain that even casual arguments for modest governmental welfare efforts this legislative season were likely to result in the advocate's being "Charles Murrayed": "The simple invocation of the book's existence will be taken as an answer to the question, even as an implied 'policy choice.' "

Probably no book of its kind in years has received so widespread media coverage. But that coverage has been a mixed blessing for Murray. Media attention does not necessarily mean accurate reporting, even for fairly sim-

Robert Royal is a research associate at the Ethics and Public Policy Center and is the editor of *Challenge and Response: Critiques of the Catholic Bishops' Draft Letter on the U.S. Economy.* His essay is reprinted by permission from the July 1985 issue of *Catholicism in Crisis.*

ple issues. Murray's book is a sophisticated statistical and social analysis of a complex and controversial subject: the negative effects of changing social mores and of federal welfare programs on the poor. As a result, many people who think they know Murray's argument only know misreadings, over-simplifications, or partisan reactions to it.

The partisan reactions were probably predictable. Conservatives finally feel vindicated, but only rarely feel moved to look carefully at Murray's analysis and to consider how it might be used to help the poor. Liberals show an equal lack of curiosity about the details of *Losing Ground* or its implications. But why have so many people found it necessary to pay attention to Murray's arguments? After all, Murray has merely buttressed an argument that many other conservatives and liberals have made for years: indulgent attitudes in the 1960s and the disincentives of several federal social programs have harmed the very poor they were supposed to help.

Even Daniel Patrick Moynihan in his Godkin Lectures at Harvard this year thought the first order of business was to dispose of Murray by cutting him down to size:

> There *are* welfare effects. Social Security probably reduces saving *some-what*; unemployment insurance probably lengthens periods of unemploy-ment *somewhat*; AFDC probably leads to more single parent households *somewhat*. But the main lesson of enquiry is that behavior is hard to explain and harder yet to modify. In this sense, *Losing Ground* is not at all a break with the past. It merely continues the practice in Washington of making large assertions with no foundations.

Moynihan then goes on to make some large assertions of his own in a credit-able attempt to defend the family. Conceding for the moment that this is a fair appraisal of Charles Murray, then how did his work ever rise to notori-ety in the first place?

The primary reasons are the sheer quality and urbane sensitivity of *Losing Ground*. The more frenetic critics seem puzzled. It is bad enough when a former grade-B movie actor or some right-wing ideologue bring criticisms of liberal programs to Washington. But Charles Murray went to Harvard, worked in Thailand for the Peace Corps and in Washington as an evaluator of federal poverty programs. He is also a sophisticated social scientist who seems genuinely concerned about the poor. Many supporters of the welfare state must have shook when they read: "Let me be quite clear: I am not sug-gesting that we dismantle income supports for the working-aged to balance the budget or punish welfare cheats. I am hypothesizing, with the advantage of powerful collateral evidence, that the lives of large numbers of poor people would be radically changed for the better." That final note of concern for the poor themselves along with the sophisticated approach have made *Losing Ground* like a fishbone in the throat for some—they cannot swallow it, but they cannot cough it out either. Murray is not easily dismissed as part of America's "new spirit of selfishness."

Furthermore, unlike many critics of the welfare system who run for cover when their data are questioned, Murray really *knows* the numbers. He has provided plausible answers to all criticisms to date. The Fall 1985 issue of the *Political Science Quarterly* will carry Murray's "A Response to the Responses to *Losing Ground*," a sober, categorical breakdown and reply to the various objections that have been raised to the book. In spite of the multiple critiques aimed at him, Murray believes that the critics have yet to lay a glove on the substance of the book. "In five or ten years after the brouhaha has died down, *Losing Ground* will be used as a textbook in statistics courses. We were that careful with the data," Murray told an interviewer recently.

Does a note of hubris enter here? No one knows for sure if he has gotten all the data right or even gotten all the data he needs. But the reply probably comes close to reflecting what both Murray and his critics sense to be the magnitude of the achievement of *Losing Ground*.

Perhaps the most striking part of the book is the opening section on the history of American sentiment about programs for the poor. Until the middle 1960s, Murray reminds us, there was a near unbroken consensus in the United States that you should not give federal welfare monies to able-bodied adults. The potential demoralization of those on the margins of the economy had already been keenly debated in nineteenth-century England. In America the fear of such demoralization remained strong. John Kennedy continued in this tradition, characterizing his anti-poverty efforts with the slogan "a hand, not a handout," a saying which resurfaced briefly at last year's Democractic National Convention. In 1963, reports Murray, even the editorial pages of the *New York Times* agreed:

> President Kennedy's welfare message to Congress yesterday stems from a recognition that no lasting solution to the problem can be bought with a welfare check. The initial cost will actually be higher than the mere continuation of handouts. The dividends will come in the restoration of individual dignity and in the long-term reduction of the need for government help.

The following year Lyndon Johnson went even further. As he signed into law some of the initial antipoverty legislation, he made sure to portray it as an end, not a beginning. "The days of the dole in this country are numbered," opined LBJ.

In hindsight, it is easy to smile at the characteristically American optimism of the Great Society programs. But we are a people who have made great strides by believing that pragmatic steps can solve any problem, and Americans had never grappled with an almost intractable problem like poverty before. Understandable optimism soon gave way to pessimism. It is important to keep in mind the professed moral views of the proponents of these early programs, because these early hopes made the failures all the more bitter. The early idealism was soon to be overwhelmed by a large shift in American self-perception.

Both the Civil Rights Movement and the Vietnam War tarnished America's opinion of itself in the 1960s. That America was morally like other nations may have been taken for granted in theory, but in practice these two historical events had profound effects on American social morale. Because America was forced to admit it had some serious flaws, suddenly it was regarded as a desperately unjust society. Individuals, especially those at the bottom of the society and the economy, were repeatedly told that they had little responsibility for their plight. Society was to blame, not only for racial discrimination, but also for poverty, poor education, criminal behavior, illegitimacy, and a host of other ills.

Large educational programs were initiated to redress the imbalances in black and other poor schools. But they were more than mere sources of funding: they changed the very nature of many schools. The result, as anyone who was teaching in the late sixties and early seventies can testify, was a drop-off in academic and behavioral standards. If bad behavior or low initial cultural levels were society's fault, you could not hold disadvantaged students up to same standards as others. In situations where poor or black students had to compete with those who were neither, the old standards would perpetuate oppression. Standards had to be lowered, a phenomenon which extended from the earliest grades to Ivy League universities.

By the late seventies many people realized what had happened, and the excellence-in-education movement slowly grew in size and momentum. But the damage had been done. Many students who would have been at the margins of the work force without the changes, left school with even worse skills and less discipline than before. A corresponding drop in job performance was only to be expected.

It is interesting to note that Murray's answer to this ongoing educational problem is some sort of voucher system. Such a system would enable the

parents of poor students who care about education—one of the surest ways
out of poverty—to fight back. Murray writes feelingly:

> Such parents have been fighting one of the saddest battles of the poor—
> doing everything they can within the home environment only to see their
> influence systematically undermined as soon as their children get out the
> door....I suggest that when we give such parents vouchers, we will
> observe substantial convergence of black and white test scores in a single
> generation. All that such parents have ever needed is an educational sys-
> tem that operates on the same principles they do.

Crime over the same period increased rapidly, arguably, says Murray, because the same kinds of attitudes came into play. Though much of America
drew the line at race riots and looting, the view about crime that gained the
most ground over the same period was that crime was not the fault of the
individual, but of society. Plea bargaining became common; a myriad of programs for offenders, especially young offenders, were set up. Jail became
thought of more as a remedial school than a place of punishment or exclusion from society. Crime rates subsequently soared.

Both of these points have often been made. But as Murray rightly adds,
the greatest losers in this whole attitudinal shift were not the middle classes.
Though middle-class students lost some ground owing to the decline in educational standards and middle-class adults certainly felt some effects of the
increase in the crime rate, by far the greatest burden of these changes fell
on the poor themselves. Permissiveness in poor schools had devastating
effects on the poor children who wanted to learn but were prevented from
doing so by disruptions or lack of academic demands. The victims of crime,
especially violent crime, were most frequently the poor, especially poor
blacks. The middle classes paid in taxes and in other ways for the new programs and attitudes, but those who paid most dearly by far were those large
numbers of poor people struggling to remain responsible and to retain
self-respect.

This is the large moral matrix in which Murray comes to the discussion
of more strictly economic factors: the effects of welfare programs on employment, poverty, illegitimacy, and families. In what follows, it will be important to keep constantly in mind that Murray is arguing that not only the actual
programs, but also the social mores described above, led to the results he
analyzes. The shifts in attitudes would have had negative effects without the
programs. The financial assistance merely enabled some of the negative
effects to merge more widely.

Losing Ground contends that the plight of the poor began to worsen in the late 1960s as the Great Society programs grew. If we take into account the nature of the economy, changes in industry, and other relevant factors during this time, claims Murray, we must find an explanation for a clear trend:

> The most compelling explanation for the marked shift in the fortunes of the poor is that they continued to respond, as they always had, to the world as they found it, but that we — meaning the not-poor and the un-disadvantaged — had changed the rules of their world. . . .The first effect of the new rules was to make it profitable for the poor to behave in the short term in ways that were destructive in the long term. Their second effect was to mask these long-term losses — to subsidize irretrievable mistakes.

Virtually every element in this argument, including the factual determination of whether the condition of the poor actually declined in the late sixties, has been under attack.

Murray extrapolates primarily from data on poor young blacks, a procedure that has caused many to accuse him of making sweeping assertions on the basis of the worst-off group in America. But he has argued in return that whenever comparable non-black groups can be statistically compared with their black counterparts, similar effects are seen. William Wilson, a black sociologist, has examined the evidence and concluded that the low educational achievement of *all* the poor seems to account for their low job achievement. Effects may thus be much more a matter of class than of race.

In order to get at the heart of *Losing Ground*, it is useful to focus on the crucial period of Murray's argument, 1965–1973, the years from the beginning of the Great Society until the oil crunch. During those years the U.S. economy was generally dynamic. In spite of the baby boom, jobs were being created faster than the baby boomers could fill them. Increased expenditures on social programs and economic growth could normally be expected to produce decreases in the poverty rate, especially since several key poverty indicators had shown steady declines since 1950 for both whites and blacks. If there are strong negative side-effects to social programs, they should be observable during these eight years.

Poverty continued to decline overall through 1973, something that Robert Greenstein, writing in the *New Republic*, offered as a refutation of Murray's thesis. Others followed suit. A writer in the *Washington Post* as late as May 1985 used this statistic to conclude flatly of Murray: "The numbers do not bear him out."

But Murray was as well aware of the numbers as his critics. His argument in *Losing Ground* was that by 1970, five years after the inauguration of the poverty programs, the decline in the rate of poverty *for working-age adults* had ceased. This qualifier is extremely important because it focuses on the group most likely to show the effects of disincentives, assuming there are any to be found. Most other analysts of the data had failed to notice that while expanded Social Security benefits continued to lessen poverty among the elderly, and certain other programs aided those who are not part of the potential workforce, the able-bodied of working age were no longer entering the economy in increasing percentages as they had for several years previously.

These negative effects were particularly strong among young blacks. During the early 1960s, the ratio of young blacks unemployed to their white counterparts was about 1.9 to 1. By 1973, the ratio had risen to 2.4 to 1. (It is worth repeating here that statistics for poor blacks may plausibly be extrapolated to other non-blacks of the same social class.) Why should this figure have risen so much?

Many critics of *Losing Ground* attribute the shift to the loss of farm jobs owing to mechanization in the South and the loss of urban minimum wage jobs to the new competition from baby-boomers and women in the North. But neither of these explanations seems to account for much. Murray examines the data carefully to show that while the sharpest decline in farm jobs occurred during the 1950s, black teenage participation in the labor force during those years did not lose ground compared to whites. As the decline lessened in the 1960s, blacks suddenly seem to be participating in labor at lower rates. Murray poses a question: "Why should a weakening 'cause' suddenly produce a new and very strong 'effect'?"

Similarly, black non-farm jobs do not seem to have been much affected by the women and others who entered the labor market in the 1960s. The low-skill, low-paying jobs that are traditionally the entry point for young blacks were simply not the kinds of jobs that the newer groups generally sought. Murray's tentative conclusion is that "young blacks changed their posture" toward such jobs. To explain this shift and some other changes in social life among the poor more concretely, it is useful to recur to Murray's now famous fictional couple, Harold and Phyllis.

Losing Ground proposes as a "thought experiment" that we try to imagine the options of a poor, average, inner-city-educated couple in 1960 and again in 1970 (after the social programs were, in full swing). This is one of the most heatedly debated parts of Murray's argument because it seeks to integrate all the previously mentioned potential causes into one snapshot view of life for those at the margins.

Harold and Phyllis have no marked skills or ambition. They dated in high school and just after graduation Phyllis finds herself pregnant. In 1960, though there are a certain percentage of common law marriages that produce technically "illegitimate" children, the moral consensus in the community is still fairly strong. Furthermore, hard work and self-respect are still largely intact values, even in the poorest communities.

Harold may or may not accept his responsibility toward Phyllis, but either way there are strict financial limits on their choices. In 1960 Phyllis will be eligible for $63 (1980 dollars used for all these calculations) per week in Aid to Families with Dependent Children (AFDC) *if* Harold does not live with her. For his part, Harold cannot benefit from Phyllis and can only find minimum wage work at $111 per week. He may not particularly like the dull hard work and low pay, but for him and for many like him hard work at such a job is the only way to move slowly up the economic ladder out of poverty. If they decide to live together, married or unmarried, they lose the AFDC payment, and only Harold's salary will be available to them, though Phyllis can also work full or part-time. Clearly in 1960 the incentives for Phyllis to live apart from Harold and to choose AFDC are not very great.

By 1970 Phyllis faces a far different financial picture. AFDC, Food Stamps, and Medicaid benefits now add up to about $134 per week. If she takes advantage of housing subsidies her prospects are even better. Assuming that she receives nothing from Harold or any other source, she is already $23 better off per week than she would have been in 1960 trying to live on Harold's salary. In the meantime, the Supreme Court has also ruled that the presence of a man in the house of an unmarried woman cannot be used as a reason to deny her benefits. Harold may now take a minimum-wage job or part-time employment and enjoy part of the total welfare package as long as he is *not* legally responsible for the child. The potential contribution of these changes to illegitimacy rates is obvious. Furthermore, community values have now also changed, making illegitimacy and dependency on welfare less of a stigma.

In fact, illegitimacy rates have been rising steadily since the 1970s. For black families in the nation, the rate is currently 55 percent, and most analysts believe that it is somewhere near 100 percent in some inner-city ghettoes. Murray characterizes the changes as follows:

> There is no "breakdown of the work ethic" in this account of rational choices among alternatives. There is no shiftless responsibility. It makes no differ-

ence whether Harold is white or black. There is no need to invoke the spectres of cultural pathologies or inferior unbringing. The choices may be seen much more simply, much more naturally, as the behavior of people responding to the reality of the world around them and making the decisions—the legal, approved, and even encouraged decisions—that maximize their quality of life.

One of the standard refutations of this explanation is that increased welfare benefits do not seem to effect illegitimacy rates directly. A 1984 Harvard study by David T. Ellwood and Mary Jo Bane found a correlation between the size of AFDC payments and living arrangements, but not between AFDC and rates of illegitimacy. Others have argued that since 1970 the value of AFDC benefits in constant dollars has dropped, yet the number of people receiving AFDC has grown slowly while the rate of illegitimate births has exploded. Again, there seems to be no causal relation between the payments and illegitimacy.

Murray himself reported in *Losing Ground* that the AFDC caseload increase during the 1950s was only 7 percent and from 1960 to 1965 only 24 percent, while it increased 125 percent in the first five Great Society years (those crucial years), 29 percent in the first half of the seventies, and only 3 percent in the second half.

But all these arguments miss the point. Murray has not argued that there is a direct ratio between benefits and deleterious social effects. Rather, his point is that there is a threshold at which percentage variations in the value of the total AFDC package do not significantly affect the decision to remain unmarried and go on AFDC, especially when doing so is an already established practice in an area.

Harold and Phyllis were located tentatively in Pennsylvania. Critics rightly pointed out that certain benefits in that state were far above those in many states around the nation and that Murray was making the decision to go on AFDC appear more attractive than it actually was in most places. But this too seems to miss the main thrust of Murray's argument. It cannot be denied that the availability of a substantial chunk of money under the circumstances outlined above will have effects on many at the margins. In 1978, for example, the General Accounting Office found that in New Orleans, a low benefit area, the monthly welfare package with housing benefits was worth $654, in San Francisco, a high area, $867. Clearly, the difference in the figures will make a difference in behavior for some, but such differences will not show an absolute statistical correlation, especially where a strong shift in attitude about welfare dependency has already occurred.

The shift in attitude about welfare dependency is also a highly disputed question. The most widely used study on welfare dependency, *Years of Poverty, Years of Plenty: The Changing Economic Fortunes of American Workers and Families*, done at the University of Michigan, reported that only 2 percent of Americans are "persistently dependent" on welfare. The U.S. Catholic bishops, for example, have used this study to object that

> One much-discussed condition that does not appear to be either a cause or a cure of poverty is personal motivation. Some claim that the poor are poor because they do not try hard enough to find a job, do not work hard enough when they have one and generally do not try to get ahead. In fact, one of the most detailed studies ever done on poverty in this country showed that initial attitudes were not an important predictor of later income. Indeed, some of those who worked the longest hours remained poor because of low wages. Until there is real evidence that motivation significantly contributes to poverty, this kind of argument should be abandoned. It is not only unsupported but is insulting to the poor [*Catholic Social Teaching and the U.S. Economy,* para. 193].

Doubtless, there is some truth to this contention and the poor should not unnecessarily be stigmatized. But the bishops and the study have to account for some other factors before reaching the conclusion they do.

To begin with, the 2 percent persistent dependency found by the study group has been characterized by Murray as a "definitional artifact." A family is classified as dependent only if it receives more than 50 percent of its income from welfare (even this excludes housing subsidies, Medicaid, child nutrition assistance, and other potential sources of income). All a family must do to fall outside this category is to earn more than the Food Stamp allowance. Persistent dependency means that a family met these specifications for eight of the ten years over which the study was conducted. Clearly, it would not take much for many families to fall outside the definition of persistent dependency while by any reasonable definition being persistently dependent. Murray points out that since 1970 at any given time a million and a half families, or about five million people, are suffering a prolonged period of at least eight years on welfare.

Part of the explanation for this problem seems to lie in the discouragement that welfare benefits give to those who can stay out of poverty only by hard work at the margins. A strawman often set up to be knocked down is that work obviously pays more than welfare and thus incentives are greater for working. Surveys of the poor show that they say they prefer work to welfare. But the subtle effects of the welfare payments may produce odd results nonetheless. Since the changes as documented above discouraged poor youth from persisting in or even obtaining low-paying jobs by making temporary periods of unemployment less burdensome, they fed into the simultaneous shifts in educational and criminal policy that produced young adults less disciplined and less prepared to become steady and reliable members of the work force, arguably with the effects on poverty, crime, and family life that have been observed.

Those who do not accept this explanation of disincentives to work, like the bishops, generally end up advocating more of the same programs to help the poor. To ameliorate these problems Murray advocates a drastic step:

> Scrapping the entire federal welfare and income-support structure for working-aged persons, including AFDC, Medicaid, Food Stamps, Unemployment Insurance, Worker's Compensation, subsidized housing, disability insurance and the rest. It would leave the working-aged persons with no recourse whatsoever except the job market, family members, friends, and public or private locally funded services. It is the Alexandrian solution: cut the knot, for there is no way to untie it.

Few may be willing to go this far with him. However it is important to note that the above paragraph specifically addresses itself to the *working-aged*. Murray immediately adds that Unemployment Insurance properly run could perhaps be brought back. He also admits that his drastic solution has no political viability, even with Ronald Reagan in the White House.

Consequently, his only reason for making the proposal at all is to underscore that eliminating federal welfare would not merely throw the poor to the wolves. It would restore positive incentives on the one hand, and on the other it would stimulate the growth of private relief institutions that have been demoralized by governmental entry into their sphere. It might also help communities virtually obliterated by the breakdown in work and family customs to rejuvenate themselves.

One of the great advantages of taking necessary relief programs out of the hands of the federal agencies and placing them in the hands of local institutions of different kinds is that it permits a flexible response to conditions. Murray may be wrong that the disincentives he identifies apply to certain communities. But he is certainly right that guidelines that must be applicable to the entire nation will never be able to take local variants into account.

Eleanor Holmes Norton, chairman of the Equal Employment Opportunity Commission during the Carter administration and currently a professor at the Georgetown University Law Center, recently wrote in the *New York Times Magazine*, "Public assistance alone, leaving people in the same defeatist environment, may reinforce the status quo. . . .The welfare program—a brilliant New Deal invention now stretched to respond to a range of problems never envisioned for it—often deepens dependence and lowers self-esteem. Although welfare enjoys little support anywhere along the political spectrum, it continues for lack of alternatives." Professor Norton differs greatly from Charles Murray in her approach to problems, especially those of the black family. It is significant, however, that even she sees the need for drastic changes in our attempt to help the poor. For blacks, she particularly underscores the responsibility that middle-class blacks have to blacks in the ghetto—a variation of Murray's emphasis on local self-help.

Many who will not be ready to accept Murray's prescriptions, like Norton, will nevertheless be ready to admit the urgency of the problem. It will be too bad if the wealth of data and the social analysis that Murray has done fall prey to partisan squabbling as is often the case in Washington. Murray has not tried to close the case once and for all, but rather to open up debate on matters that have long lain unexamined. Furthermore, he is not alone in his analysis. Credible work along similar lines has been done by George Gilder, Ken Auletta, Douglas Glasgow, John Langston Gwaitney, and others. Liberal commentator Nicholas Lemann, while by no means accepting everything Murray has to say, justly summed up the current situation in his remark that Murray's is "a vision that coheres, as the left's on this subject doesn't anymore."

Given the nature of the case, it is probably impossible to prove in scientific fashion that Murray is right—or wrong. A human being behaves in odd ways and for motives that are obscure even to himself, let alone to the social scientists. Integrating such psychological quirks with the complex changes that occur in a society over a particularly unstable period like the past twenty years may well require something approaching omniscience. Murray's partly justified confidence in his numerical analysis notwithstanding, more persuasive accounts of the same two decades may lie just over the horizon.

If nothing else, however, *Losing Ground* has made a strong plea that we take the negative effects of our good intentions seriously, not merely dismiss such effects as inevitable by-products of large scale-solutions. These by-products are crucial to the moral health and very lives of a significant segment of the American people. After *Losing Ground*, warnings about the moral costs of social programs can no longer be ignored as a manifestation of lack of concern for the poor. Charles Murray may or may not be right that we have lost ground since 1965, but he is certainly right that we must think with more care and with greater imagination if we wish to gain ground in the future.

The Moral Quandary of the Black Community

GLENN C. LOURY

THE CIVIL RIGHTS MOVEMENT now confronts its greatest challenge – to redefine an agenda created during the turbulent 1950s and 1960s, so that it may conform with the socio-political realities of the coming decades. The central theme of this essay is that the redefinition should be centered around an effort to expand the range of activities that directly seek to mitigate the worst conditions of lower-class black life.

A long tradition of philanthropy and internally directed action aimed at self-improvement exists among black Americans, pre-dating the emancipation. The Urban League, a major civil rights organization today, was founded early in this century to help new black migrants from the rural South adjust to life in Northern cities. Similarly, black fraternal and professional organizations, through a wide array of programs and activities, have been "giving something back to the community" for decades. Yet the nature of problems facing the black community today, the significant recent expansion of opportunities for blacks in American society, and the changing political environment in which black leaders now operate, all dictate that greater stress should be placed upon strategies which might appropriately be called "self-help."

For notwithstanding this noble tradition of mutual concern, the dominant tendency among today's public advocates of black interests is to emphasize the responsibility of government to resolve the problems of blacks. To be sure, policies of local, state, and federal government significantly affect the welfare of black Americans. And no one would deny, in turn, that blacks have the right and responsibility to participate in shaping those policies. But it is now beyond dispute that many of the problems of contemporary black

Glenn C. Loury is a professor of political economy at Harvard University. This essay is reprinted with his permission from the Spring 1985 issue of *The Public Interest*.

American life lie outside the reach of effective government action, and require for their successful resolution actions that can be undertaken only by the black community itself. These problems involve at their core the values, attitudes, and behaviors of individual blacks. They are exemplified by the staggering statistics on pregnancies among young, unwed black women and the arrest and incarceration rates among black men. Such complicated problems, part cause and part effect of the economic hardship readily observed in the ghettoes of America, defy easy explanation. These problems will not go away with the return of economic prosperity, with the election of a liberal Democrat to the presidency, or with the doubling in size of the Congressional Black Caucus.

The fact is, any effective response to such difficulties will necessarily require the intimate involvement of black institutions, politicians, educators, and other concerned individuals, and far more attention than is now received from these quarters. My concern is that too much of the political energy, talent, and imagination abounding in the emerging black middle class is being channeled into a struggle against an "enemy without," while the "enemy within" goes relatively unchecked.

Fault vs. Responsibility

Some may object that problems of family instability and crime are themselves manifestations of oppression—the historical and ongoing racism of the "enemy without"—and that to focus on self-help strategies aimed at the behavior of blacks is to treat the symptoms of oppression, not its causes. If jobs were provided for those seeking work, the argument continues, and if a commitment to civil rights could be restored at top levels of government, these internal problems would surely take care of themselves.

I believe this argument to be seriously mistaken, and under certain circumstances possibly quite dangerous, for it invariably ends by placing the *responsibility* for the maintenance of personal values and social norms among poor blacks on the shoulders of those who do not have an abiding interest in such matters. It is important to emphasize, however, that in rejecting this argument, I am not questioning the existence of a link between behavioral difficulties on the one hand, and the effects of racism on the other. To the extent that, say, the percentage of black children raised in single parent homes is greater because black men are denied employment opportunities, one could correctly conclude that the problem has been caused by the racist denial of opportunity. One might, then, assign blame or *fault* to racist whites, to the extent that their racism can be determined in this way to have caused certain difficulties among blacks.

Even so, this argument founders, in my view, when on the basis of presumed fault it assumes a concomitant responsibility to resolve the difficulties which have emerged. As Orlando Patterson has brilliantly argued, fault and responsibility must not be presumed to go hand-in-hand. It is absolutely vital that blacks distinguish between the fault which may be attributed to racism as a cause of the black condition, and the responsibility for relieving that condition. *For no people can be genuinely free so long as they look to others for their deliverance.*

The pride and self-respect valued by aspiring peoples throughout the world cannot be the gift of outsiders — they must derive from the thoughts and deeds of the peoples themselves. Neither the guilt nor the pity of one's oppressor is a sufficient basis upon which to construct a sense of self-worth. When faced with the ravages of black crime against blacks, the depressing nature of social life in many low-income black communities, the alarming incidence of pregnancy among unwed black teenagers, or the growing dependency of blacks on transfers from an increasingly hostile polity, it is simply insufficient to respond by saying "This is the fault of racist America. These problems will be solved when America finally does right by its black folk." Such a response dodges the issue of responsibility, both at the level of individual behavior (the criminal perpetrator being responsible for his act), and at the level of the group (the black community being responsible for the values embraced by its people).

Consider, as an illustration of this point, a recent public statement made by thirty prominent black leaders and intellectuals on the problems of the black family:

> No strategy designed to improve the status of black Americans can ignore the central position of the black family as the natural transmitter of the care, *values*, and *opportunities* necessary for black men, women, and children to reach their full potential as individuals [*A Policy Framework for Racial Justice,* Joint Center for Political Studies; emphasis added].

Thus there is clear recognition that values and opportunities available only within families, and unavailable to many blacks, play a crucial role in determining individual achievement. This is a welcome observation, too seldom seen in the public pronouncements of black leaders. But in the very next sentence responsibility for this state of affairs is laid at the door of American society:

> The present black family crisis, characterized chiefly by the precipitous growth of poor female-headed households, can be traced almost directly to American racism. . . . As large numbers of blacks migrated to large cities from rural areas, black males have often been unable to find work, and government policies and other social forces further sapped family strength. These trends proceed apace today, aided by the widespread failure even to recognize the pressures on the black family as central to other problems, and by the failure to devise both preventive and healing strategies.

It is clear from the context that the "failure" being discussed is that of "racist American society," not of the political, intellectual, and religious leadership of the black community itself, which might more appropriately be regarded as responsible for the normative health of the group. Certainly one can trace some of these family difficulties to American racism. But having recognized this, it is crucial that we confront the question of how to change the behavior of the young blacks raised in such families. Whatever *fault* may be placed upon "racist American society," the *responsibility* for the behavior of black youngsters lies squarely on the shoulders of the black community itself.

There is potential for great danger in ignoring this responsibility: Those who may be legitimately held at fault for the black condition may nonetheless fail to act to improve that condition. It seems increasingly obvious that the animating spirit of the Great Society era, during which government took seriously the responsibility to help solve the problems of the black poor, is on the wane. Those who proclaimed the enormous stake of the black community in preventing the re-election of Ronald Reagan must now confront the implications of his landslide victory. It is by no means certain that the leaders of either party will in the years ahead continue to have an expansive sense of government obligation to the black poor. John Jacobs, president of the National Urban League, recently stated the problem quite clearly:

> We see the problems facing black families as being problems facing our nation. But the nation is not addressing those problems. The Administration and the Congress have cut lifeline programs that help all poor people and especially poor black families. They have drastically cut programs that help poor children survive — including nutrition and health programs. . . . Given that failure to act, we feel that the network of black institutions must play a greater role both in the advocacy on behalf of the black family, and in concrete programmatic ways that provide aid to black

families – assistance to help two-parent families stay intact, resources to help single-parent families survive, and programs that help our children to take their rightful place in our society. We are confident that the black community has the institutional and voluntary resources to be effective in this great task.... For every element of our society must deal with that aspect of the problem for which it is best suited.... That means government must be supportive, black institutions must marshal volunteer resources, *and individual black people must accept responsibility for themselves* and for preserving the family values that helped us to survive [*The Urban League News,* April 1984; emphasis added].

Jacobs is keenly aware of the dangers of inaction in an indifferent, if not actually hostile, political environment. By stressing his confidence in the ability of blacks to grapple with these profoundly difficult problems, he by no means absolves the larger society of its obligations. He recognizes, however, that ultimately it is the leaders of the black community, himself among them, who are responsible for addressing these problems.

A New Frontier

The effort of such organizations as the National Urban League to come to grips with these internal difficulties suggests a new direction for the institutional and intellectual resources of the black community (and, more generally, the civil rights community). It is now two decades since the enactment of the Civil Rights Act of 1964, and some thirty years since the landmark *Brown* decision was rendered by the Supreme Court. These and other monumental achievements of the Civil Rights Movement are, for the current generation of American youth, the stuff of history books. Today's young people have no recollection of the struggles. The crowning achievements of an earlier era dwarf in significance anything likely to issue from the litigation and lobbying efforts of today's advocates. In other words, the civil rights strategy – seeking black advancement through the use of the legal system to force America to live by its espoused creed – has reached the point of "diminishing returns." It is no exaggeration to say that we now live in the "post-civil-rights" era.

Yet, if one were to poll the community of activists, lawyers, politicians, and concerned citizens whose effort made "The Movement" a reality, a sizeable majority would, I believe, say that the work they began remains seriously incomplete. They would point to the significant economic inequality which remains between the races in the United States. A growing percentage of

black children are living below the poverty line; the prisons of the country
are disproportionately populated by black men; black families are more often
dependent on public assistance than the population as a whole; and residential
segregation by race is a commonplace in our central cities, as is the racial
segregation of public schools which so often accompanies it. Moreover, it
would be observed that overt expressions of racism have not yet vanished
from the American scene. Thus, it would be argued, much on the civil rights
front remains to be done.

Nevertheless, it is much easier to assert that something must be done than
it is to set out an agenda for action. Many veterans of the movement find
themselves today in the position of sensing how crucial it is that action be
taken, and yet not quite knowing what to do. *I suggest that the next frontier
for the movement should be a concerted effort to grapple directly with the
difficult, internal problems which lower-class blacks now face.* In the post-
civil-rights era, the energy and imagination of the individuals and organizations that achieved prominence in the struggle for civil rights may be most
usefully employed in efforts to confront those serious internal difficulties
which beset our low income black communities.

It is important to avoid misunderstanding here. I do not suggest that black
advocates abandon their traditional concern with the issues of desegrega-
tion, equal employment opportunity, or voting rights. There is important work
to be done in these areas, even if it consists mainly in defending past gains.
But a realistic assessment of the prospects of the poorest black Americans
strongly suggests that their lives will not be profoundly altered by the continued pursuit of historically important civil rights strategies. In central-city
ghettoes across America, where far too many young black mothers struggle alone to raise the next generation of black youth, it is difficult to see the
potential for fundamental change via these traditional methods. Even the
election of black candidates to the highest municipal offices has so far failed
to effect such change. Yet, to the extent that we can foster institutions within
the black community that encourage responsible male involvement in parent-
ing, help prevent unplanned pregnancies, and support young unwed mothers
in their efforts to return to school and become self-supporting, important
changes in the lives of the most vulnerable segment of the black population
can be made.

These ought not to be seen, then, as mutually exclusive strategies. Financial
and other government support may aid internally directed action of the sort
described above, and this action will certainly be more effective as the

elimination of historical forms of discrimination takes hold. Moreover, the traditional civil rights organizations are especially well situated to undertake these internally directed efforts: They have a strong network of affiliated local organizations, a reputation for service to the black community, the ability to call upon the most talented and accomplished individuals within the black community for assistance, and they continue to enjoy the respectful regard of many in the philanthropic institutions.

Political Discourse and Self-imposed Censorship

The undertaking which I advocate — centered, as it is, on the behavior of individuals — will necessarily involve a discussion of values, social norms, and personal attitudes. Such an undertaking is a difficult matter at best, and especially so in recent years for black Americans. Black leaders and intellectuals have, on the whole, sought to avoid public discussion of the role that such normative influences might play in the perpetuation of poverty within the group. This is understandable but unfortunate, because there really is no other way in which such matters can effectively enter public discussion. For government to attempt in the name of public policy to mandate, or even to discuss, what the values and beliefs of any segment of the society should be, is to embark on a course fraught with political, constitutional, and moral pitfalls. Moreover, in today's political climate, concerned external observers of the black community are in no position to raise such issues if they desire to maintain their credibility as "liberals." Only blacks can talk about what other blacks "should" do, think, or value and expect to be sympathetically heard. That is, *only blacks can effectively provide moral leadership for their people.* To the extent that such leadership is required, therefore, it must come from within.

Even so, such leadership has been in relatively short supply. While black communities and their residents have been dramatically affected by "black-on-black" crime (many inner-city merchants now offer their goods from behind bullet-proof partitions, and black ghetto-dwelling women face a risk of rape higher by several magnitudes than that faced by whites), black congressmen concerned with criminal justice issues focus instead on "police brutality." Although police behavior is obviously an issue of legitimate concern to blacks, the damage done by the criminal element within black communities should be regarded as an even greater concern. As the gap in academic achievement between black and white youngsters persists at intolerably high levels, very little can be heard from black leadership (with a few noteworthy exceptions) regarding the extent to which this performance gap is the result of the behavior and values of black children and their parents. As black women struggle to provide for themselves and their children without appropriate financial support from their men, discussion of male irresponsibility has been largely confined to the writings of black feminists.

This is a curious situation, for individual middle-class blacks have long emphasized and lived by values and norms that are entirely inconsistent with the behavior described above. Such behavior is thus not only inconsistent with success in American society, but also with the ethos of much of the black community itself. Current and future black spokesmen and leaders are drawn almost exclusively from this social stratum. But having achieved professional success, they appear not to recognize that their own accomplishments are rooted in the kind of personal qualities that enable one best to take advantage of the opportunities existing in American society. As a result, the opportunity for their lives to stand as examples for the lower class of the community goes relatively unexploited.

A moment's reflection on the history of black Americans will suggest why the discussion of values and norms has been such a limited part of the group's struggle for social advance. Obviously, the atmosphere of racist ideology within which blacks have had to function is of fundamental importance. Since the early days of slavery, and owing to the justification necessary for its practice in a democratic, Christian society, blacks have been forced to defend their basic claim to an equal humanity before the general American public. The presumed inferiority of the African was the primary rationalization of his enslavement. The social Darwinists of this century and the last, by finding the explanation of blacks' poverty in their culture or genes, posed basic challenges to the integrity and self-respect of the group. The "retrogressionists," who well into this century argued that the black population was doomed to revert to its natural state of depravity without the civilizing influence of paternalistic masters, created an environment for thoughtful blacks that has been unique among American ethnic groups.

Among the major consequences of this ideological environment is the stifling effect that it has had on the internal intellectual life and critical discourse of the black community itself. Objective assessment and discussion of the condition of the community has been made difficult for blacks because of the concern that critical discourse within the group (about the problems of young, unwed mothers, or low academic performance, for example) might be happily appropriated by external critics seeking support for their base hypotheses.

It is hard to overstate the significance of this constraint on discourse among blacks. Its consequences have not gone unnoticed by outside observers. As Daniel P. Moynihan once wrote regarding his earlier study of the Negro family:

> It is now about a decade since my policy paper and its analysis. As fore-casting goes, it would seem to have held up. . . .This has been accompa-nied by a psychological reaction which I did not foresee, and for which I may in part be to blame. . . .I did not know I would prove to be so cor-rect. Had I known, I might have said nothing, realizing that the subject would become unbearable and rational discussion close to impossible. I accept that in the social sciences some things are better not said ["The Schism in Black America," *The Public Interest,* Spring 1972].

Moynihan, of course, had argued that the growth of single-parent fami-lies posed an emerging and fundamental problem for blacks that would impede the ability of some to advance in the post-civil-rights era. It is by now quite evident that he was right. The problem he identified nearly twenty years ago is today twice as severe, with no solution in sight. And yet, when he released his study he was savagely attacked for "blaming the victim," and for failing to see the inner strengths of these families whose form represented a necessary adaptation in the face of American racism.

A similar scenario could be offered to describe the reaction of some black leaders to discussions of racial difference in arrest and incarceration rates for various criminal offenses. The NAACP apparently views this disparity as further evidence of inequality of opportunity:

> Blacks make up only 12 percent of the nation's total population. . .but an incredible 50 percent of the total prison population. With half of all the prisoners in the United States being black, the fact that only 4 percent of the nation's law enforcement personnel is black is a sad commentary on equality of opportunity. . . .Why are so many blacks in prison? And why are so few blacks in law enforcement? One inescapable answer applies to both questions: Racism. Superficially, it would appear that blacks com-mit more crimes than anyone else. . . . [However] [t]he only explanation for this. . .discrepancy is conscious choices of key decision-makers to focus on crimes committed more frequently by blacks [*The Crisis,* April 1982].

The intellectual perspective evident in these remarks clearly precludes any serious discussion by black leaders of the problem of criminal behavior. It is incredible, in light of the obvious consequences for those who must live in the crime-ridden neighborhoods of our central cities, that organizations dedicated to improving the welfare of blacks are so reluctant to oppose this behavior forthrightly. There are worse things than "blaming the victim."

One could also mention discussions in the social science community of racial difference in performance on intelligence tests, which elicit a similar reaction from black leaders. All of these problems—family instability, criminal behavior, academic performance—have these features in common: They are essential if one is to understand accurately the condition of the black population; their resolution is fundamental to the progress of blacks; and they are seized on as evidence by those outside the black community who subscribe to racist propositions about black inferiority. As a result, many blacks have imposed on themselves a kind of censorship; they agree not to discuss these matters frankly in public and to ostracize those blacks who do.

One can generalize about the source of this difficulty. Political discourse within a somewhat insular and legitimately suspicious community requires trust. The nature of the external threat is such that members of the community must always be "on guard." There are those who would welcome proof of the group's inferiority, rationalize its predicament, or roll back its progress. These forces may have supporters, witting or not, within the group itself, and members of the group know that their every public utterance must be calculated with this in mind. One cannot know with certainty, then, where a speaker is "coming from," but this in no way inhibits speculation as to his motives. Someone who speaks on behalf of the "free market," or who intimates that there are deep structural problems within black communities having to do with values and attitudes, courts trouble because enemies of the group have made similar claims. In such an environment it is likely that individuals within the community will tacitly agree not to discuss certain ideas, at least not publicly, thereby impoverishing political discourse.

Tacit censorship of this sort tends to perpetuate itself, and for good reason. Once it exists, suspicion of those who violate the implicit accord becomes justifiable; for in a sense, the accord acts like a self-fulfilling prophecy. Only someone who places relatively little weight on social acceptance by the community—someone who, therefore, is objectively less likely to share the group's prevailing conception of its interests—would be willing to breach the implicit contract of silence. Self-imposed limits on the group's discourse might, then, live on after most individuals have recognized that something is wrong.

This suggests that when the barriers to discussion finally break down, as they must, the change will be both rapid and complete. Because of their unimpeachable integrity and commitment to the community, such institutions as the black churches, fraternal and sororal organizations, and the nationally based civil rights organizations are particularly well suited to this undertaking. While the behavioral problems described here are by no means unique to blacks, the stifling of critical discourse within the black community has impeded analysis and slowed the development of new approaches to resolve these problems.

Black Political Capital

The fact that values, social norms, and personal behaviors often observed among the poorest members of the black community are quite distinct from those characteristic of the black middle class indicates a growing divergence in the social and economic experiences of black Americans. The extent and importance of this divergence is often the subject of acrimonious debate, but its existence is beyond serious dispute. The simple fact is that the opening of opportunities occasioned by the legal and political successes of the Civil Rights Movement has led in a generation's time to a dramatic increase in the number of blacks attending elite colleges and universities, entering the professions, and engaging in successful business enterprises. Yet the ghetto-dwelling residents of central Harlem, of Watts, of the west side of Chicago, or of the east side of Detroit are not often found among this new cadre of aspiring young blacks. Nor is the prospect that their children will enter this social stratum nearly as great as it is for black children elsewhere. There are thus genuine differences in the social circumstances of blacks, differences which suggest the much abused sociological concept of "class."

These differences in social circumstance, together with the realities of political advocacy on behalf of blacks in contemporary American life, provide a compelling *moral* argument for the expansion of internal actions aimed directly at improving the circumstances of the black poor. The point is that more fortunate blacks benefit, through the political system, from the conditions under which the poorest blacks must live. This implies a concomitant obligation to help improve those conditions, though there may be little incentive to do so.

The methods by which blacks wield influence on the formulation of public policy in this country are legion. There is, of course, the effect of the ballot. Many Southern politicians have learned to "sing a different tune" because of their recognition that election without black support has become impossible. In major urban areas throughout the country black candidates now successfully compete for the highest offices, significantly affecting the conduct of local governments. The 1984 presidential campaign suggests additional channels through which the black vote can influence policymaking.

In addition to raw political muscle, however, blacks enjoy the benefit of the widely (though, obviously, not universally) held perception that their demands on the political system are a test of its justice and fairness. The extent to which an administration is perceived as "sensitive" to the claims of blacks has become a measure of its compassion, or a sign of its callousness. Many Americans accept the notion that the government should, in some way, deal with the problems of blacks because that is the proper and decent thing to do. The existence of "liberal guilt" has been instrumental in sustaining political support for initiatives of substantial benefit to blacks.

There are few things more valuable in the competition for government largess than the clearly perceived status of victim. Blacks "enjoy" that status by dint of many years of systematic exclusion from a just place in American life. A substantial source of influence thus derives from the fact that blacks are perceived as having been unjustly wronged and hence worthy of consideration. *The single most important symbol of this injustice is the large inner-city ghetto, with its population of poor blacks.* These masses and their miserable condition sustain the *political capital* that all blacks enjoy because of their historical status as victims.

The growing black "underclass" has become a constant reminder to many Americans of a historical debt owed to the black community. Were it not for the continued presence of the worst-off of all Americans, blacks' ability to sustain public support for affirmative action, minority business set-asides, and the like would be vastly reduced. (Even women's groups, by citing in support of their political objectives the "feminization of poverty"– a phenomenon substantially influenced by the increasing number of black families headed by women with low incomes – derive benefit from this source.) The suffering of the poorest blacks creates, if you will, a fund of political capital upon which all members of the group can draw when pressing racially based claims.

It is thus not surprising to find that whenever any black leader argues for special assistance to some members of his community, whether that assistance flows directly to the poorest blacks or not, one will hear about the black teenage unemployment rate or the increasing percentage of blacks living below the poverty line. The fact that the median black family income has increased little relative to white family income over the period 1960–1980 is frequently cited by black spokesmen and others to support the general claim that "nothing has changed." No major government purchasing effort at the local, state, or federal level can proceed now without the question being raised "What is in this for minority business?" Inevitably the low economic status of the black poor will be referred to as justification for the claim.

I am saying nothing here about the motives of black leaders, businessmen, or professionals. I only observe that their advocacy for policies that benefit blacks who are not themselves poor is most effective when couched in terms that remind the American polity of its historic debt, and that this is most readily accomplished by referring to the condition of the poorest blacks.

And how have the black poor benefited from the policies extracted from the system in their name? The evidence suggests that, for many of the most hotly contested public policies advocated by black spokesmen, not much of the benefit "trickles down" to the truly poor. As far as I know, there is no study to support the claim that set-asides for minority-owned businesses have led to a significant increase in the level of employment among lower-class blacks. It is clear from extensive empirical research on the effect of affirmative action standards for federal contractors that it is mainly those blacks in the higher occupations who have gained from this program. If one examines the figures on relative earnings of young black and white men by educational class, by far the greater progress has been made among those blacks with the most education. Looking at relative earnings of black and white workers by occupation, one finds that the most dramatic earnings gains for blacks have taken place in the professional, technical, and managerial occupations, while the least significant gains have come in the lowest occupations, like laborer and service worker. Thus, a broad array of evidence suggests that better-placed blacks have simply been able to take better advantage of the opportunities created in the last twenty years than have those mired in the underclass.

The Marxian notion of exploitation refers to a circumstance in which workers receive less from the process of production than their labor has contributed. It seems evident that today poor blacks gain less from the political process than their votes and misery contribute to the effectiveness of black advocacy. Sadly, this circumstance may continue for some time.

I am not suggesting any malice or bad faith on the part of middle-class blacks who are able to extract concrete gains from the system. Indeed, these individuals need not realize how their behavior, along with that of many others, leads to a situation in which exploitation occurs. It seems to be a feature of the contemporary American political economy that the kind of benefits most readily generated for blacks accrue more often to those who are not worst-off. It is a simple matter to see that the prime contractor on a large municipal construction project uses a certain percentage of black sub-contractors, and much harder to assure that the fatherless child of a poverty-stricken mother avoids the hazards prevalent in the ghetto. We can demand that a consumer franchise company give dealerships to black entrepreneurs, but not that the high school valedictorian be black.

This, to my mind, is solid basis for a moral argument that ways must be sought to enlist those blacks who have achieved a modicum of security and success in the decades-long task of eradicating the worst aspects of black poverty. The nature of the problems besetting inner-city communities, the character of political advocacy by blacks in the post-civil-rights era, and the drift of politics in contemporary America seem to require that any morally defensible and realistic program of action for the black community must attend first to the fostering of a sense of self-confidence and hope for the future among members of the black "underclass." Certainly, the federal government can play a critical role in this process. Yet it is equally clear that the black business, academic, and political elites must press for improvement in their own peoples' lives, through the building of constructive, internal institutions, whether government participates or not.

Toward a Family
Welfare Policy

Michael Novak

IN AMERICAN POLITICS, there is no longer any argument of principle between the major parties concerning two propositions: (1) Every citizen of the United States is entitled to the opportunity to improve his or her condition; and (2) there must be a floor or safety net providing at least the rudiments of decent living conditions under every citizen.

In this respect, basic Catholic social teaching has been in principle vindicated within the American system. This is not to say that important debates do not remain or that the agenda for action has been fulfilled. It is only to say that, on these two propositions at least, agreement in principle has been reached. Debate now centers on the *design* of actual programs and the probable consequences of alternative designs, not on the matter of principle.

Furthermore, a capitalist economy, a democratic political system, and a pluralistic Jewish-Christian moral-cultural system—the three-systems-in-one which constitutes democratic capitalism—properly provide for the welfare of dependent and needy persons. It is not only consistent with, but incumbent upon, a democratic capitalist society to "promote the general welfare" through care for the less fortunate. Those on the left tend to turn for such care to the state; those on the right tend to turn for such care to the private sector. Such differences afford much controversy and political struggle. But the disputes center on the means, not on the goal. The view is almost universal that something is desperately wrong with the present design. The so-called Tarrytown Group of black scholars recently declared, e.g., that welfare programs for poor mothers particularly "need to be completely reconceptualized and redesigned."[1]

Michael Novak, a well-known Catholic layman and prolific author, holds the George Frederick Jewett Chair in Religion and Public Policy at the American Enterprise Institute. This essay is reprinted by permission from *Catholic Social Teaching and the U.S. Economy* (© 1984 by University Press of America, Lanham, Maryland).

The Catholic bishops of the United States, therefore, have an opportunity to help imagine a better future. Which principles of the Catholic tradition offer light to guide future public welfare policy? Three such principles seem especially promising: the building of intact families; what the Vatican calls "self-reliance"; and subsidiarity. Such principles could establish a new course for U.S. public policy.

A new course is surely needed. In 1959, 23 percent of poor families were headed by females. In 1982, after billions of dollars of welfare programs and the massive efforts of the War on Poverty, and after welfare expenditures in 1980 *twenty-one times* the levels of expenditures in 1950,[2] the proportion of female-headed households in poverty had increased to 48 percent.[3] This destruction of families is unprecedented. The Catholic tradition cannot possibly be used to defend it. What is wrong? What needs to be changed in the *design* of public policy?

Furthermore, despite immense and unprecedented expenditures to eliminate poverty, the poverty level in the United States hit its lowest historical plateau at 11 percent in 1973, climbed back up to 13 percent in 1980, and to 15 percent in 1982.[4] The sums of money being spent to eliminate poverty exceed by far the sums necessary to lift every man, woman, and child in the United States above the poverty line. Something clearly absurd is going on.

It might be well, then, to look closely at the official description of the poor in the United States to gauge the nature and dimensions of the problem. Then we shall turn to the Catholic traditions for light on how problems of need and dependency might be susceptible of social solution. It is my intention, above all, to stress the importance of *family* welfare policy. This primary strength of Catholic social teaching has never, so far, been utilized in U.S. social policy.

The Poor and the Disadvantaged

According to the Census Bureau Report for 1982, some 34 million persons in the United States have an income below $9,862 for a non-farm family of four. This figure does not include any of the non-cash benefits (food stamps, housing aid, Medicare, and the like) received by such persons. Not counting non-cash benefits, the total *cash* income reported by the poor—not enough to lift them out of poverty—comes to $55 billion.[5] Half of all poor households received at least $6,477 in 1982 as cash; half received less.[6] Put another way, the *poverty short-fall*—the amount that would have been needed to raise the cash-income of all over the poverty line — came to approximately $45 billion.[7] Viewed in itself, this is not an insuperable amount. It may be compared to annual expenditures for social services in the federal budget (not counting social service expenditures by the states, and not counting assistance from private sources) of $390 billion in 1982.[8]

As these figures show, an annual grant, totaling about $45 billion would suffice to eliminate poverty as a monetary matter. Yet significantly more than this amount is already being *targeted* for the poor. Consider the following estimated expenditures in FY 1983 (ending September 30, 1983).[9]

Food stamps	$12.0 billion
Housing assistance	9.3 billion
Aid to Families with Dependent Children	7.8 billion
Women, infants, and children	1.1 billion
Low Income Energy Assistance	1.8 billion
Child nutrition	3.2 billion
Supplemental Security Income	8.8 billion
Medicaid (federal; does not count state)	19.3 billion
Unemployment benefits	36.9 billion
Earned income tax credit	1.2 billion
TOTAL	101.4 billion

One may not conclude from these figures that the poor in the United States are adequately cared for. What one must conclude is that sufficient federal funds are being expended to have lifted every man, woman, and child in the United States above the basic poverty level of $9,862 for a non-farm family of four.

It is clear from these figures that if poverty were merely a matter of dollars, the actual cash earnings of the 34 million poor plus the amounts already expended by the federal government in their assistance would have already eliminated poverty in the United States. Our eyes tell us this is not the case. But before delving deeper into the problems of the poor, it is well to see from the Census Bureau reports just who they are. The following table illustrates their profile.[10] It reveals that only 19.4 million of the poor are between the ages of 16 and 64. Of these, nearly 3.4 million are living at home with small children. Another 3 million of the poor are ill or disabled. Thus, only about 13 million of the poor are potentially able to work. Of these, 9 million worked for pay during at least part of 1982.[11]

THE POOR IN THE UNITED STATES, 1982
(In Thousands)

Total poverty population, 1982	34,398
Children under 15	11,587
Persons over 65	3,751
Young singles (16–24)	1,349
Other adults (25–64)	18,012
Persons living alone	6,458
White	23,517
Black	9,697
Hispanic	4,301
Single female head of households (number of households)	3,434
−Same, including children	11,286
Ill or disabled	2,809
Looking for work	1,327
Located in Northeastern states	6,364
North Central states	7,772
Southern states	13,967
Western states	6,296
Outside metropolitan areas	13,152
Inside metropolitan areas	21,247
Inside central cities	12,696

This brief survey shows that the vast majority of the poor are truly dependent. Through no fault of their own, most are not, and cannot be, self-reliant. Other studies show that *individuals* typically move into and out of the poverty ranks with considerable volatility. A study by the University of Michigan showed that only 17 percent of the poor (in the ten years surveyed) had been in poverty for as long as two years running. Poverty for most, the researchers conclude, tends not to be a permanent condition. Individuals in vast numbers fall into it temporarily and rise again. (Many graduate students, numbering 1.6 million nationwide, can testify to that.[12]) This is important in countering the myth of "a permanent underclass."[13] Many of the poor are temporarily down on their luck, and help received can start them on an upward path again.

There are two schools of thought on the problem of poverty. One argues in dollar terms chiefly. The point is simply to give money to the poor and stop worrying. The second is that poverty is not primarily a money problem but a problem dollars alone cannot solve. It is a problem of human potential (the economists say "human capital"). Many of the poor, especially among the young, need help in learning skills and attitudes: how to read, how to apply for and hold a job, how to govern themselves and conduct themselves. Self-reliance is a virtue of many parts, according to this view, and it can be taught. This is especially true of youths currently unprepared for employment, the so-called "unemployables" who even if they get a job do not long hold it.[14] Modern society demands skills in nutrition, child care, literacy, and techniques of many kinds (driving a car, making purchases, preparing a résumé, expressing oneself clearly) which are not given automatically but must be learned. Indeed, the term "disadvantaged" points in part to this aspect, suggesting that not all persons start out with the same advantages.

It is crucial to note here that some persons even of an earlier aristocracy or proper middle class may now be as financially poor as church mice, without being "poor" in social class; while some financially poor persons are "bourgeois" in their virtues and attitudes.[15] In this sense, the "advantages" of a certain culture are not coincident with financial status. The problem of poverty is, therefore, quite different when it is only a question of income and when it is a question of skills. Many Americans can well remember being very poor, in the sense of having a very low income, without ever having felt "poor," in the sense of being culturally disadvantaged.

This is an important point. For church bodies can do a great deal about the moral-cultural dimension of poverty which mere money cannot do. It would be naive to believe that money is always an incentive to "lifting oneself out of poverty." Money can subsidize habits which lead to demoralization. This assertion is subject to empirical testing. In a section of downtown Albany, persons today classified as poor have financial resources far exceeding (even correcting for inflation) the resources of families who lived there in preceding generations; simultaneously, they suffer from far higher levels of violence, demoralization, and despair than were ever known there before.[16]

We are accustomed to talking about poverty in pious tones which are blind to its awful reality. For often what we are talking about is not the relative absence of money but the psychological destructiveness felt by individuals. These feelings may not arise from free will; indeed, those possessed of them feel victimized. This is a spiritual, not an economic disease. Some share it who—as dope dealers, thieves, prostitutes, or pimps—have income far above the national median. There is a moral dimension to poverty—what

Kenneth Clark has described as its "pathology"[17] — of which churchmen, above all, are aware.

The vast majority of the poor, as Census Bureau figures show, are white. Many such persons (like many in all races) do not "feel" poor. Some live largely outside the cash economy, needing to purchase only those things they do not produce for themselves. Some live as they do in order to be self-reliant. A cash income of $9,862 a year in 1982 did not seem to many in the small towns of America a "poverty income" or a cause for desperation.

It may be well to sum up the material so far.

First Thesis: In every society, a certain percentage of persons (the too young, the too old, the disabled, mothers with small children) are not capable of economic independence but are dependent on others; in a good society, such persons must be cared for.

Second Thesis: In the United States, poverty short-fall (1982) amounted to between $43–45 billion; this represents the cash income needed to lift all persons above the official poverty line of $9,862 for a non-farm family of four. This is not a socially insuperable amount; in fact, more than that amount is already being spent in federal assistance alone (not counting state, local, and private efforts).

Third Thesis: Clearly, the mere supplying of "the poverty short-fall" through monetary grants would not solve the problem of poverty, since poverty is not merely a matter of dollars only but also has a moral-cultural dimension, usually captured by the modifier "disadvantaged." Economic sufficiency and independence depends on health, skills, and attitudes; lack of these constitutes "disadvantage."

From these three theses, two social policy decisions seem to follow. (1) Those of the poor (especially the young) who possess the health, skills, and attitudes necessary to achieve self-reliance need to be assisted by programs which *empower* them but *do not generate dependency.* (2) Those of the poor who lack the skills and attitudes necessary for self-reliance require special assistance. In this second arena, the churches can make a unique contribution.

Beyond finite limits, the church cannot give dollars or provide more than modest material assistance: food lines, used clothing, and the like. Some forms of poverty are not psychologically destructive; many persons have been poor without pathology. Yet the evidence is overwhelming that some portion of the poor is suffering from demoralization and self-destructive behavior.[18] Unless church leaders address this core problem — a problem of the moral-cultural dimension – they turn away from their proper task. For this is a problem in which the state has no special competence and in which great expenditures by the state appear, by the evidence, to be making matters worse.

Consider the devastation to the family which appears to accompany certain specific federal expenditures (i.e., Aid to Families with Dependent Children, but not all). The integrity of the family is a primary issue of social justice. It is one of the main justifications for the concern of the churches about poverty. If poverty made no spiritual difference, especially to the families, the churches would have little cause to be concerned with it. What can the Catholic church do for poor families?

A National Family Policy?

One of the deepest and best of all Catholic social traditions is its concern for the integrity of the family. The family, in Catholic social thought (and in virtually universal judgment), is the basic social unit. Modern Anglo-American thought has tended, however, to pay disproportionate attention to "the individual" (the conservative pole) and "the state" (since 1935 the liberal pole[19]). The individual and the state were the two novel realities of modern times. For the rise in individual opportunity liberated the human person from the fixed status of birth and family heritage, which had governed feudalism. And the rise of the modern nation state overrode the social forms of the feudal era. In this shift of attention to the individual and the state, the fundamental importance of family was typically not so much denied as ignored – although not so in Catholic social thought.

It may not at all have been an accident, then, that President John F. Kennedy, in his budget message of 1962, laid down as the first principle of a sound welfare policy (the first step toward President Lyndon Johnson's "War on Poverty") that "it must stress the integrity and preservation of the family unit." Similarly, concentration on the family has been a preoccupation of Senator Daniel Patrick Moynihan.[20] Recent publications of the National Association for the Advancement of Colored People and the Civil Rights Commission have also begun to pay close attention to the deterioration in the families of those parts of the population most affected by welfare programs since 1962.[21]

The irony is clear. Welfare programs whose first criterion in 1962 was to "stress the integrity and preservation of the family unit" seem to be correlated with precisely the reverse results. Devastating results have been experienced in white and Hispanic welfare families and even more devastating results in black families.

In 1960, before the federal government became involved in the "War on Poverty," single white mothers with dependent children constituted 6.0 percent of all white families with children, while the equivalent figure for black families was 20.7 percent. By 1970, these percentages had grown to 7.8 percent and 30.6 percent, respectively. By 1980, they had leapt again: to 13.4 percent and 46.9 percent.[22] Clearly, each time many of these mothers have another child, the poverty figures will rise. Each poor young girl aged fifteen to nineteen who has a child will also add to the figures. The birth rate among poor teenagers keeps growing.[23]

In 1982, the proportion of poor persons was 15 percent of the total population. But if single mothers with dependent children had remained at the same rate as in 1960, the proportion of poor persons would fall to 13.0 percent (from 34.4 million to 29.9 million).[24] This is in part because intact husband-wife families among blacks between the ages of 25–34 have income levels at 89 percent of similar white couples.[25] Of the 9.6 million blacks who are poor, almost half (4.6 million) are in female-headed households. This portion of the poverty population continues to grow at a rapid pace. The following table illustrates the composition of the black poor.[26]

POVERTY AMONG U.S. BLACKS, 1982
(In Thousands)

	ALL BLACKS	BLACKS BELOW POVERTY LEVEL	
All blacks	27,216	9,697	35.6%
Under 18	9,401	4,472	47.6%
22–64 years	13,458	3,578	26.6%
Over 65	2,124	811	38.2%
Black families	6,530	2,158	33.0%
Married couple families	3,481	543	15.6%
Female householder, no husband present	2,734	1,535	56.2%

These figures show clearly that the presence of both a mother and father in the home is the most certain road out of poverty. Only 15.6 percent of such black families are poor. On the other hand 56.2 percent of black female-headed families are poor. In short, the "integrity and preservation of the family unit" of which President Kennedy spoke in 1962 does seem to work as a way out of poverty. But whatever is causing the growth in female-headed households is slowly multiplying the numbers of the black poor: more than 1.5 million female heads of households and approximately 3 million children, nearly half the black poor, fall in this growing class.[27] This is a human-made tragedy, caused by neither nature nor nature's God. It should not be beyond the wit of humans to halt what they have set in motion.

Catholic social teaching offers no pat remedy for this problem. It does command the Catholic conscience to attend to it. To assert merely that the federal government should distribute more benefits to single mothers with dependent children is not likely to lead to a decrease in the number of single-parent mothers and their dependent children. On the contrary, the number seems to be increasing from decade to decade in correlation with the advent of social welfare programs designed, purportedly, for the opposite effect. Something seems wrong in the design.

It seems worth pausing to mention that a similar deterioration is taking place in white and Hispanic welfare families. Of the 5,118,000 white families who are poor, 1,813,000 (35 percent) are headed by a female householder, no husband present.[28] Of the 916,000 Spanish-origin families who are poor, 425,000 (46 percent) are headed by a female householder, no husband present.[29] These numbers, too, keep growing.

Unless welfare programs arrest the growth in female-headed families, no husbands present, it seems certain that the numbers of the poor will continue to grow in future years. In 1982, the largest single category of the poor was single mothers and their dependent children. Their total number came to 11.3 million, or 33 percent of all poor persons.[30]

Furthermore, a growing percentage of children every year are being born illegitimate. In 1970, e.g., the percentages of illegitimate births were: among whites 5.7; among blacks 37.6. By 1980, these percentages had climbed to 11 and 55.2 respectively.[31] Worse still, between 1970 and 1980 the proportion of illegitimate births among women aged 15–19 rose from 17 to 33 percent among whites and from 63 to 85 percent among blacks.[32]

Questions of poverty, therefore, are today inextricable from questions of family life. The so-called "feminization of poverty" is, as the figures show, mostly a problem of abandoned single women, many of whom have never formed families.

Moreover, this deterioration in the struggle against poverty is growing just as progress is being made in other areas. In 1959, 35 percent of the elderly were poor.[33] By 1982, advances in Social Security (especially in indexing payments to inflation) had lowered this to under 15 percent, and non-cash programs like food stamps, housing assistance, and Medicare had ameliorated the lot even of these.[34] Similarly, poverty rates for intact husband-wife families had been lowered considerably, although much remains to be done. Finally, the numbers of adult poor persons living alone had been lowered to just under 6.5 million.[35]

The great disappointment has been with regard to family life. There welfare programs have seemed to have perverse effects, exactly opposite to those intended. Since so many children are involved, and since a sizeable proportion of their young mothers are not much more than children, the problem is heart-rending and acute.

What is to be done? There can be no doubt that assistance must be provided. Aid to Families with Dependent Children (AFDC) is a relatively small portion of the federal welfare budget. In 1982, it came to $8.2 billion.[36] Typically, AFDC checks are paid directly to the young mother. So are other forms of assistance, including food stamps, housing assistance, Medicaid, and the like. These grants paid directly to the woman make her dependent upon the state rather than upon the father of her children. The incentive for males to take responsibility for their own children is bypassed. The state, feeling no requirement to intervene in matters of morality, may simply mail a check. But this act seems counter to all known systems of social morality and social accountability, and counter to family morality as well. So what is to be done?

Imaginative social philosophy is clearly called for. The United States remains virtually the only welfare state not to have in place a family welfare policy. No doubt, the received intellectual tradition of concentrating either on the individual or on the state, while ignoring the family, has had a profound effect upon public policy. Yet the Catholic tradition clearly teaches that the welfare of families—Kennedy's "integrity and preservation of the family unit"—is paramount in all schemes of social justice. What would be a fresh Catholic response to the existing problems of care for the needy and dependent in American social policy?

A Fresh Start: A Family Welfare Policy

The 1919 statement by the United States Catholic bishops was far in advance of its time. It is the same sort of imaginative leap that seems called for in our present circumstances. The criteria for a new social welfare policy issued by the bishops should be three: that it be distinctively Catholic; that it meet an urgent social need; and that it be – in the long run, if not the short – workable or at least worth working towards.

Reflection on the current poverty population of the United States reveals that the vast majority of the needy – some 28 million – live in families. Thus, a welfare policy designed explicitly for families would go a very long way toward ending (or seriously alleviating) poverty in the United States. Secondly, reflection on "the poverty short-fall" in 1982 shows that the *financial cost* of a family welfare policy ought not to be prohibitive. This is particularly true if the new policy were to replace the present confusing, overlapping "welfare mess." Finally, from all sides, conservative and liberal, cries for welfare reform coincide with visible exhaustion concerning how to bring it about. These three factors suggest that a new design is worth working towards and, in time, may prove highly practical.

So let us begin with the children first. The best circumstance for infants and the young is an intact family, with both mother and father present. If social policy desires something as the circumstance, it should reward it. Therefore, social policy ought to provide child allowances to parents of intact families. Parents serve the common good by the care they bestow on their children. In the United States in 1982, there were 49.6 million intact families, with a total of 25.3 million children. There were 3.8 million intact poor families with a total of 7.6 million poor children.[37] Clearly, the latter population needs help more than the whole range of families. On the other hand, political action is often easier if its base is as inclusive as possible. So it is with Social Security.

Thus, two principles come into conflict: (1) to help the neediest; (2) to treat all equally. Usually, a compromise is possible. Thus, one can imagine *larger* child allowances to the neediest, and *smaller* allowances above certain income levels. One way to do this would be to treat child allowances as taxable income, in such a way that those whose income is below the poverty level are exempted from taxation and those above it are taxed at proportionate rates.

A non-farm family of four in 1982 required a cash income of $9,862 to be classified as non-poor. In 1982, all poverty families together numbered 7.5 million.[38] If such families had earned no income at all, the maximum cost of full income support would be less than $75 billion ($9,860×7.5 m.). This sum by itself would in that case eradicate poverty as a monetary matter. But of course no such sum would be needed, since most poor families, and especially intact families, already have considerable cash income. The shortfall, as we have seen, is closer to $45 billion. It seems plausible that a child allowance of $150 per child per month or $1800 per year would suffice to raise a large majority of intact poor families above the poverty level.

It may not be wise to attach numbers to these matters at this early stage. The public policy principle is to devise a system of social welfare which stresses "the integrity and preservation of the family unit." The point is to achieve two goals at once: to alleviate (or eliminate) poverty while simultaneously rewarding intact families, in the hopes of generating more of them. Perhaps one cannot solve the *whole* problem of poverty. But if one could lift out of poverty the 3.8 million intact families who were poor in 1982 (together with their approximately 7.6 million children), one would have dramatically reduced the dimensions of poverty. The total cost of such an effort in 1982 would have been $14 billion ($1800 × 7.6 m. children) — slightly larger than the food stamp program.

What about the remaining poor families, those headed by single mothers? Such persons, numbering 11.3 million mothers and children, are often in desperate need; many of the mothers are teenagers themselves (often enough the daughters of mothers who began life the same way). The problem for public policy has three parts: (1) to help such women and their children, in such a way that they may escape from dependency; (2) to avoid having the state assume responsibilities which properly belong to the fathers of children; and (3) to avoid supplying unintentional incentives to others who might choose to follow this path. It is not easy to meet all three criteria.

Despite the rapid growth in the number of abortions among the poor, by 1980 55 percent of all births to black women were of fathers unknown to the law, up from 38 percent in 1970.[39] This immense flight of males from the most basic responsibility of manhood is both a social and a moral catastrophe. But what the state can do about it is unclear. Making welfare checks payable directly to a young woman, especially in the thirty-one states which require the absence of any male, seems clearly to be an incentive to male irresponsibility. It may be wrong to involve the state in questions of marital status; but the claim to assistance based upon marital status does so involve it. For this reason, it seems important that, at least for younger women, state assistance should neither be nor seem to be an incentive to male irresponsibility.

Having a child outside of wedlock, furthermore, should be looked at as a matter not solely of morality but also of social consequences, one of which may be dependency upon the state. May the society not exact costs in return? Socially burdensome behavior must be discouraged, just as socially beneficial behavior should be rewarded. Are there devices open to a good and generous society which might meet the required criteria? Social thinkers have been hesitant in approaching this matter, as well they should be. Their hesitancy is a contributing factor to the growing incidence of female-headed households in poverty.

The children in such households are already penalized by the lack of a father to guide their steps, to supply a masculine discipline and presence, and to help prepare them for the social economy. They need assistance in overcoming these disadvantages, as well as those of poverty itself. This the state alone can hardly supply.

It thus becomes clear that the poverty which results from single-parent households is a problem demanding social action on a scale larger than that available to the state alone. Moral and cultural institutions must play a role. So must the media. So also the schools, families, neighborhood groups and associations of every sort.

This effort will require moral leadership. For having children out of wedlock, or abandoning a woman and the child one has fathered, are not afflictions which fall from the skies but are consequences of voluntary human behavior. The Catholic bishops could provide significant leadership in convening a broad-based coalition of church leaders, media elites, and social workers to support poor persons in non-formed families and in families broken by widowhood or divorce. For example, on each local level, leagues of female-headed households could be formed under the auspices of local churches, neighborhood associations, and voluntary organizations. The idea would be to have local persons who know the heads of households personally become the administrators of social assistance. There is reason to believe that the vast majority of female-headed families are found in cities and towns, in which local organizations already flourish. No new bureaucracy would have to be created. Rather, the good works of such organizations could be sharply focused upon assistance to needy families. Such assistance would have personal as well as monetary dimensions.

Furthermore, AFDC and other forms of federal and state assistance would then be channeled through local family centers. Checks would not be distributed directly to individuals below the specified age (age 20), but only through the sponsoring organizations. It would be more useful for federal funds to be paid to urban churches, for example, to maintain day-care centers for children and learning sessions for young heads of households, including meal service, than to give the funds to individuals. The point is to use the financial power of the state to strengthen the local networks whose personnel know the needy personally, and to spend funds in such a way that the educational assistance they provide *empowers* the needy to begin, at a later stage, to care for themselves. In this way, state assistance need not lead to dependency upon the state, but to personal empowerment.

The moral principle is that state power must not be used to create dependency, but rather to empower local social organizations to meet genuine social needs and to empower needy individuals to acquire the skills of self-reliance.

A summary of Catholic family welfare policy for the needy would, therefore, be as follows:

1. Child allowances would be paid on a monthly basis to husband-wife intact families. These funds would count as taxable income. Those families below the poverty level would not, of course, pay taxes. Indeed, families up to one hundred percent above the poverty line (approximately the median income level) might be exempted.

2. For non-formed families and families broken by abandonment, separation, divorce, and death, for heads of households below the age of (say) twenty, federal and state assistance would not be paid directly to the needy but, rather, to local family centers which would provide child care, instruction, and meals.

These two steps should provide two considerable steps forward. First, a significant percentage of intact families now in poverty should be lifted out of poverty by step one. Second, the cycle of dependency would be ameliorated by personalized local assistance and educational programs aimed at self-reliance.

These programs would not alone eliminate all poverty. But by concentrating on family strengths they would significantly diminish the numbers of intact families who are poor. They would also provide, as it were, local surrogate extended families for non-formed and broken families. These alone would represent great steps forward for millions from among the poor. Immediately, they should reduce the impersonal dependence of non-formed and broken families on government checks, while providing significant personal and financial assistance.

The Family in Catholic Social Thought

In 1920, John A. Ryan quoted with approval the statement of an Inter-denominational Conference of Social Service Unions in Great Britain, which "points out that all social reform must take as its end and guide the maintenance of pure and wholesome family life."[40] Similarly, many years later, Bishop von Ketteler, whom Pope Leo XIII described as a major founder of modern Catholic social thought, held that the chief fault of German liberalism was its opposition to "the divine plan for the procreation and education of men by means of the family."[41] Indeed, it was concern for the family, the cradle of all human morality and spirituality, that justified for Leo XIII papal attention to the problems of social reconstruction. This tradition is summarized very clearly by Pope John XXIII in *Pacem in Terris* (para. 16):

> The family, grounded on marriage freely contracted, monogamous and indissoluble, must be considered the first and essential cell of human society. To it must be given, therefore, every consideration of an economic, social, cultural, and moral nature which will strengthen its stability and facilitate the fulfillment of its specific mission.[42]

Pius XII, celebrating in 1941 the fiftieth anniversary of *Rerum Novarum*, calls attention to "the three principal issues of social life in economic affairs, which are mutually related and connected one with the other, and thus interdependent: namely, the use of material goods, labor, and the family."[43]

One of the very strongest texts of the Catholic tradition, however, is found in *Rerum Novarum* (para. 10):

> For it is a most sacred law of nature that a father must provide food and all necessaries for those whom he has begotten; and similarly, nature dictates that a man's children, who carry on, as it were, and continue his own personality, should be provided by him with all that is needful to enable them honorably to keep themselves from want and misery in the uncertainties of this mortal life. Now, in no other way can a father effect this except by the ownership of profitable property, which he can transmit to his children by inheritance. A family, no less than a State, is, as we have said, a true society, governed by a power within itself, that is to say, by the father. Wherefore, provided the limits be not transgressed which are prescribed by the very purposes for which it exists, the family has, at least, equal rights with the State in the choice and pursuit of those things which are needful to its preservation and its just liberty. . . .We say, at least equal rights; for since the domestic household its anterior both in idea and in fact to the gathering of men into a commonwealth, the former must necessarily have rights and duties which are prior to those of the latter, and which

rest more immediately on nature. If the citizens of a State—that is to say, the families—on entering into association and fellowship, experienced at the hands of the State hindrance instead of help, and found their rights attacked instead of being protected, such associations were rather to be repudiated than sought after.[44]

This text powerfully underlines the emphasis on families and their associations suggested in the proposal of local family centers independent of state bureaucracy mentioned above.

Allan Carlson, in an important article, has pointed out that the cultural system of democratic capitalist societies powerfully inhibits naked individualism. He writes: "The natural unplanned genius of the new order lay in the cultural forces which kept this destructive consequence of liberal-capitalism in check. *The first of these was the family*."[45] Jewish-Christian sexual and family teaching is a crucial component of the holistic liberal sensibility; emphasis on family is central to the American ethos. He continues:

> The creative social bond between morality and modern family was particularly strong in the United States. Tocqueville noted that although European visitors to America disagreed on many points, they all concurred that moral standards were far stricter in this country than elsewhere. He attributed this to the unique balance of freedom, equality, and responsibility found in the American marriage covenant.[46]

Catholic social teaching, clearly, recognizes that the family is the essential, fundamental unit at whose integrity and fruition wise social policy should be aimed. Indeed, were there to be a conflict between the will of the state and the good of families, the Church would clearly be bound to side with the latter. Thus, United States social welfare policies for the poor must be scrutinized in the light of the good of families. In this respect, President Kennedy's criteria for a sound welfare reform were sound: "It must stress the integrity and preservation of the family unit. It must contribute to the attack of dependency, juvenile delinquency, family breakdown, illegitimacy, ill health, and disability."

No one can correctly say that the people of the United States are not spending through their government enough money to have eliminated poverty. For the total sum of money needed to bring the 7.5 million poor families in the United States (1982) to $10,000 per year is $75 billion, far less than is currently being spent. Neither can anyone correctly say that the current *design* of U.S. public policy for the poor is meeting the criteria President Kennedy set for it in its beginnings.

Here is where the Catholic bishops have an *opportunity*. Given the emphasis of Catholic social teaching on family welfare, they have the possibility of offering some badly needed originality. In the past, conservatives faced with a problem have typically turned to the *individual*; liberals faced with a problem have turned to the *state*. Neither solution, time has shown, meets the tests of reality. In drawing the attention of the public policy community to the *family*—a mediating structure *between* the individual and the state—the Catholic bishops could propose a new public policy agenda as wide reaching for the next fifty years as the New Deal was for the past fifty. The role of the state is to *empower* people, not to make them dependent.[47] The institution designed by nature to empower them, above all, is the family. The programs of the state should be designed to strengthen families. For strong families provide the surest and most direct path out of poverty, and are nature's own institutional means for providing adequate income to the poor and the needy.

Catholic social policy differs from traditional American conservatism (at least of the libertarian type) by holding that the state must play a role in helping the needy. It differs from traditional American liberalism by holding that state assistance which generates dependency violates the principle of subsidiarity; that the family is prior to the state; and that the family is prior to the individual as the focus for social policy. In all these respects, Catholic social policy has an opportunity to establish new directions, at a moment when new directions are universally desired.

NOTES

1. See Judith Cummings, "Breakup of Black Family Imperils Gains of Decade," *New York Times,* November 20, 1983.
2. Charles A. Murray, *Safety Nets and the Truly Needy: Rethinking the Truly Needy* (Washington, D.C.: Heritage Foundation, 1982), p. viii.
3. David O'Neill, "Poverty and Use of Clever Slogans," *Washington Times,* November 24, 1983, p. 1C. The devastation of the black family is especially evident. The Census Bureau reports: "The number of poor Black families with a female householder rose from 834,000 in 1970 to 1.4 million in 1981. These families accounted for 70 percent of all poor Black families in 1981, substantially up from 56 percent in 1970." U.S. Bureau of the Census, *America's Black Population: 1970 to 1982,* Special Publication PIO/POP-83-1 (Washington, D.C.: 1983), pp. 4, 9.
4. U.S. Bureau of the Census, *Statistical Abstract of the United States: 1982–83,* 103d ed. (Washington, D.C.: 1983), table 727; *Money Income and Poverty Status of Families and Persons in the United States: 1982,* table B.
5. Telephone inquiry, U.S. Bureau of the Census, October 6, 1983; figure from unpublished Current Population survey.

6. See *Money Income and Poverty Status of Families and Persons in the United States: 1982,* table 20.

7. Spencer Rich, " 'Poverty Gap' Put at $45 Billion," *Washington Post,* October 19, 1983, p. A6. Testimonies of Rudolph G. Penner, director, Congressional Budget Office, and Sheldon Danziger, Institute for Research on Poverty, University of Wisconsin, to the House Ways and Means Committee, October 18, 1983.

8. Office of Management and Budget, *Payments to Individuals,* February, 1983.

9. Office of Management and Budget, *Outlays for Social Programs,* February 1, 1983.

10. *Money Income and Poverty Status of Families and Persons in the United States: 1982,* table 14. Testimony of David A. Stockman, director, Office of Management and Budget, before the House Ways and Means Subcommittees on Oversight, and Public Assistance and Unemployment, November 3, 1983, p. 4.

11. Ibid., table 17.

12. National Center for Education Statistics, *Opening Fall Enrollment,* 1982 (unpublished).

13. See Ken Auletta, *The Underclass* (New York: Random House, 1982).

14. "If poverty and lower-class existence are viewed as *structural* patterns, caused by a poor distribution of skills, jobs, income, and the like, then the remedy is apparent: expand lower-class blacks' access to these resources. If, on the other hand, lower-class existence is viewed more broadly, as a function of cultural patterns, then the remedy is far more elusive and problematic. For then the difficulty becomes one of devising solutions that simultaneously correct maladaptive cultural patterns (delinquency, crime, unwed motherhood, street-corner lifestyles, drugs) and those structural deficiencies or institutional inequities (inflation, recession, unemployment, poor schools, and the like) that shrink opportunity for the poor.... Allies of the black lower class must devise ways and means for reducing certain cultural or societal pathologies widely prevalent among lower-class blacks. Lower-class lifestyles among young men and women that are associated with the 'man-child' and 'woman-child' syndrome—above all, becoming mothers and fathers while still in one's teens—must be interdicted, constrained, and reversed." Martin Kilson, "Black Social Classes and Intergenerational Poverty," *Public Interest,* LXIV (Summer, 1981), pp. 68–70.

15. "Class may (or may not) find phenomenological expression, but at root it is a mode of self-definition. These are aristocrats in England who are as poor as church mice but are definitely 'upper class.' And there are immigrants to the United States who are also poor as church mice but definitely 'middle class' from the moment they set foot here. The very thought that there is someone ('up there?') who knows better than we do what class we are in is as breathtaking in its intellectual presumption as it is sterile for all serious purposes of social research." Irving Kristol, *Reflections of a Neoconservative* (New York: Basic Books, 1983), pp. 199–200. See the whole of chap. 14, "Some Personal Reflections on Economic Well-Being and Income Distribution."

16. See George Gilder, *Visible Man* (New York: Basic Books, 1978).

17. See Kenneth B. Clark, *Dark Ghetto* (New York: Harper and Row, 1965). See esp. chap. 5, "The Pathology of the Ghetto," pp. 81–110. "The dark ghetto is institutionalized pathology; it is chronic, self-perpetuating pathology; and it is the futile attempt by those with power to confine that pathology so as to prevent the spread of its contagion to the 'larger community.' Not only is the pathology of the ghetto self-

perpetuating, but one kind of pathology breeds another. The child born in the ghetto is more likely to come into a world of broken homes and illegitimacy; and this family and social instability is conducive to delinquency, drug addiction, and criminal violence" (p. 81).

18. See Auletta, op. cit.

19. See John Dewey, *Liberalism and Social Action* (New York: Capricorn Books, 1963).

20. See Daniel Patrick Moynihan's introduction to Alva Myrdal, *Nation and Family* (Cambridge, Mass.: MIT Press, 1968).

21. See, for example, United States Commission on Civil Rights, *A Growing Crisis: Disadvantaged Women and Their Children,* Clearinghouse Publication 78, May 1983.

22. *Statistical Abstract of the United States: 1982–83,* table 73.

23. "Prior to 1970, women 15 to 19 years old had less than half of all illegitimate births. By 1975, as a result of decreasing illegitimacy rates at older ages and increasing rates among women 15 to 19 years old, teenage women accounted for more than half of all illegitimate births." U.S. Bureau of the Census, *Perspectives on American Fertility,* Series P-23, No. 70 (July, 1978), pp. 40–41. From 1975 to 1979, the number of births to unmarried women aged 15–19 increased by 14 percent, from 222 per 1,000 to 253 per 1,000. See *Statistical Abstract of the United States: 1982–83,* table 97.

· 24. Calculated from *Money Income and Poverty Status of Families and Persons in the United States: 1982,* tables 14–15. As a proportion of the total poverty population, female heads of households with their dependent children virtually doubled between 1960 and 1982, climbing from 15 percent to 29 percent. Despite a reduction in the total number of poor children, from 17.3 million in 1960 to 13.1 million in 1982, the number of poor children in families headed by females increased from 4.1 million to 6.7 million during the same period of time. See ibid., tables 14–15.

25. United States Department of Commerce News, CB 83-127, August 22, 1983.

26. *Money Income and Poverty Status of Families and Persons in the United States: 1982,* tables 14, 17–18.

27. Ibid., tables 15 and 18.

28. Ibid., table 18.

29. Ibid.

30. *New York Times,* Sunday, November 27, 1983. Testimony of David A. Stockman, op. cit., table 1, p. 4.

31. National Center for Health Statistics, *Monthly Vital Statistics Report,* Advance Report of Final Natology Statistics, vol. XXXI, No. 8 (November 30, 1982).

32. Ibid.

33. *Money Income and Poverty Status of Families and Persons in the United States: 1982,* table 15.

34. Ibid.

35. Ibid., table 14.

36. U.S. Executive Office of the President, Office of Management and Budget, *Budget of the United States Government, Fiscal Year 1984,* p. V-125.

37. U.S. Bureau of the Census, Current Population Reports, series P-20, No. 381, *Household and Family Characteristics: March 1982* (Washington, D.C.: 1983), table 5; *Money Income and Poverty Status of Families and Persons in the United States: 1982,* tables 14–15.

38. Ibid., table 18.

39. *America's Black Population: 1970 to 1982*, p. 20.

40. John A. Ryan, *Social Reconstruction* (New York: Macmillan, 1920), p. 222.

41. L. Lenhart, "Ketteler, Wilhelm Emmanuel von," *New Catholic Encyclopedia* (New York: McGraw-Hill, 1907), VIII, 170.

42. *Seven Great Encyclicals* (Glen Rock, N.J.: Paulist Press, 1963), p. 292.

43. Ibid., p. 227.

44. Ibid., p. 6.

45. Allan C. Carlson, "The Family and Liberal Capitalism," *Modern Age*, Summer/Fall, 1982, p. 366.

46. Ibid., p. 369.

47. Peter L. Berger and Richard Neuhaus, *To Empower People* (Washington, D.C.: American Enterprise Institute, 1977).

An Alternative Vision of the Welfare State

PETER L. BERGER

THE TOPIC OF the welfare state is rather dismal, and not only in right--of-center circles. In American English the phrase has attained a particularly pejorative connotation, because "welfare" has come to mean the dole, handing out public money to people, many of whom may not deserve it. It is perhaps salutary to recall that, originally, the phrase was a very positive one. As far as I know, it originated in Bismarck's Germany; the English phrase is a literal translation of the German *Wohlfahrtsstaat.* Bismarck (not exactly a left-winger) introduced the first modern welfare-state measures for what, in all likelihood, were mixed motives — because he wanted to steal the thunder of the growing socialist movement, but also because, in the best Lutheran tradition, he sincerely believed that the community must be responsible for those in need and that, under the new conditions brought about by industrialism, some of this communal responsibility fell to the state. In this country, of course, the welfare state came much later — basically, in two big spurts, in the 1930s and 1960s. Whatever may be one's criticisms of the American welfare state, it seems to me important to recognize, and indeed to reaffirm, the moral convictions that inspired its establishment. The most important of these convictions is that a society should be judged by the manner in which it treats its weakest members. And both Bismarck and the New Dealers were quite right that, in a modern industrial society, at least some of the responsibility for the weak must fall to the state.

The complete, or even near-complete, dismantling of the welfare state and the turning over of all, or most, social services to private institutions is neither politically realistic nor morally desirable. Also, it is quite unnecessary to deny that the welfare state, in this country and elsewhere, has indeed

Peter L. Berger is University Professor at Boston University. This essay is reprinted with his permission from the November 1983 issue of *Catholicism in Crisis.*

resulted in important benefits to many weak sectors of society. These benefits, however, have been obtained at very high costs. A realistic and morally defensible agenda is to restructure the welfare state in such a way as to maintain its benefits while reducing its costs.

The *economic* costs of the modern welfare state have become all too obvious, and indeed have become a major political issue in every Western democracy. The same issue has been one of the most important factors behind the turn to the right in many of these democracies. This is fine. What is less fine is that, in consequence, right-of-center parties and governments have projected an image of cost-cutting meanness, while their left-of-center opponents have paraded under the banner of the "party of compassion." It is essential, therefore, to stress that the economic costs are not the only costs of the welfare state as we now know it. There are very important social and human and indeed moral costs, which may seem less urgent but which in the long run are even more serious than the economic costs. What are these costs? They have been the establishment of vast bureaucratic and professional empires, with a state-enforced monopoly over social services. Those who receive the services have become disenfranchised in terms of their autonomy as human beings, converted into "clients" in the full original sense of that word (which, in Latin legal terminology, meant a dependent individual). This dependency has perverted both public and private morality, fostering a climate of irresponsibility and resentment.

What this adds up to is that the *present system should be changed even if it were less costly in money terms.* The changes that, in my opinion, are called for would, very probably, cost less money. This may be a case of virtue being rewarded. But these changes would be commendable even if the money costs remained the same or even if they were higher. It is both politically and morally essential that those of us who understand the failures of the welfare state categorically refuse to concede to the other side the label "party of compassion." Leave aside here the arrogance of the notion that compassion can be neatly categorized in ideological terms; let it be stipulated that individuals who genuinely care for their fellows can be found at all points of the political spectrum. More importantly, it is hardly compassionate to keep going a welfare system that wrecks the economy, especially as the poor and other weak members of society are the ones who suffer most from this wreckage. *That*, indeed, is a point often made on the right, and it is a valid one. But there is another, exceedingly important point to be made: It is also not very compassionate to provide people with services, especially with services that they really need, at the price of their autonomy and self-respect. The goal of a humane social policy must be to provide the necessary services, but at the same time to protect and to expand the control that the recipients have over their own lives. As any psychologist can tell us in terms of individual life, there is compassion that stifles and there is compassion that empowers. The same is true of society. If a label is required, I would suggest we call ourselves *the party of empowerment.*

Such sentiments can become items for campaign rhetoric of right-of-center parties. But, given the dynamics of democracy, political gains in the very short run can come only from rhetoric that has no concrete content in terms of practical policies and legislation. Let me, therefore, talk very concretely about the new model of the welfare state that some of us have been talking about for some time (and let me say at this point that such a new model is what is clearly indicated by the innovative thinking that has been initiated by Robert Woodson and his associates at the National Center for Neighborhood Enterprise).

Obviously, I have neither the time nor the competence to spell out such a model in any detail. Equally obviously, no one, I think, can claim at this time to know exactly and in every detail what such a model will eventually look like. To work out these details is precisely the practical agenda that, I believe, is before us. But there are a number of quite concrete criteria to apply as we go about constructing this new model. Without claiming these to be exclusive, let me suggest four.

One: *Government should empower people to take control of their own lives even as it provides services to meet specific needs.* Or minimally: *Government should not, in providing services, take away such control as people do have over their lives.*

For example (and it is a very crucial example), if there is one power that virtually all people want, all over the world and in every group, it is the power to control the values instilled in their children. Indeed, this power is a fundamental human right. Now, those who are poor or otherwise handicapped in the exercise of parental responsibility may have to turn to the state for help in meeting the needs of their children – for education, health care, nutrition, and for other services. It is intolerable that all too often the state will provide these services only if, in effect, parents surrender the power over the process by which values are instilled in their children. To be sure, some of these services are provided by the state for the poor and the more affluent alike – such as education via the public school system. But the more affluent parents always have the option of obtaining the services elsewhere – in this case, by sending their children to private schools. It is poor parents who are "clients" of the public education system, which, *for them*, is a coercive monopoly, and which very frequently represents values that they strongly disapprove of.

Two: *As far as possible, recipients of government-supplied social services should have a choice among suppliers.* Put differently: *As far as possible, suppliers of social services should be forced to compete with one another for the favor of recipients.*

Monopolies corrupt. Monopolies fix prices. This is true in the overall economy; it is equally true in the economy of the welfare state. Thus there is every reason to believe that introducing competition among suppliers of social services will reduce money costs. But, just as important, individuals who have a choice also have their self-respect enhanced. They are changed from "clients" to consumers. They are enfranchised to shape their own lives in whatever area they have options. Let me return to the previous example. More affluent parents are consumers of educational services, and by virtue of this fact they are in a position to exercise considerable influence over the schools they elect to patronize. Poor parents do not have this option. It seems to me that it should be an important purpose of social policy to redistribute this particular power in society – that is, to use public resources to give poor parents a comparable range of choices. An additional point should be made here: *In terms of empowerment, choice is almost always better than participation.* Leave aside the fact that most so-called participation is window-dressing; think here of parent-teacher associations in inner-city school districts. But even if participation is real, how many parents (especially poor parents) have the time and energy to participate fully in the shaping of a school program? The choice to go to *another* school is vastly more empowering.

Three: *Those who provide social services should be accountable to those who receive the services.*

Again, what is at issue here is a redistribution of power over one's own life. An upper-income person will speak of "my doctor" or "my lawyer," and this phrase will refer to social reality to the extent that the cash-for-service arrangement does bring about at least a measure of accountability. Important point: There is nothing anti-professional, or even anti-bureaucratic, in insisting on such accountability. It is not a question of denying respect to professional expertise where it applies, or of some utopian goal of abolishing modern bureaucracy. Rather, the social purpose here is to make both professionals and bureaucrats exercise their undeniable talents in the service of independent and uncoerced people, instead of making people the passive objects of professional and bureaucratic ministrations.

And fourth: *Social policy should respect the pluralism of values and lifestyles in American society.*

Pluralism in some degree is the hallmark of every modern society; it is one of the major characteristics and strengths of American society. Social policy should employ this strength, not try to weaken it. It is *not* the purpose of social policy, whether in education or in any other area, to impose on everyone the values and lifestyles established in the white, college-educated, upper middle class. There have been all sorts of complaints—some coming from the left and some from the right in conventional political terms—that this sort of imposition is going on. I would suggest that most of these complaints have been perfectly justified. So with the complaints of blacks that social workers are trying to apply alien standards to the lives of black families. So with the complaints of evangelicals that educators are trying to indoctrinate their children with a secularist worldview. And so on.

So much for these four criteria (or, if you prefer, principles) that, I believe, are useful to assess social policies—and, by the same token, draw a very rough outline of the new model of the welfare state. Now let me be a little more concrete. All of this adds up to what I believe should be a central feature of the new model: *As far as possible, social services should be delivered by mediating structures, or minimally, with their cooperation.* Put differently: *Mediating structures should be the centerpiece of the new model of the welfare state.* What does this mean?

I ask your indulgence; I know that some of you have heard this before; it bears repeating. "Mediating structures" sounds like just the sort of terminological monster only a sociologist could think of (and I plead guilty, with due apologies to the language of Shakespeare and Milton). But the reality that this term refers to is very well known and crucial in most people's lives: Mediating structures are those institutions that *stand between* the individual and the enormous (mostly bureaucratic) structures of a modern society, and especially between the individual and the state. The most important of these institutions are the family and organized religion. Then there is the (often informal) network of institutions engendered by the local community or neighborhood. And then (last but not least) there is the world of voluntary association, with its vast array of institutions expressing the common purposes and values of different groups of people. We call these institutions "mediating" because they act as bridges between private and public life. They express the personal values and identities of individuals, but at the same time they relate these individuals to public purposes.

I have been convinced for about a decade now that mediating structures are the secret of viability of a modern society, especially if that society is democratically governed. In 1977 Richard Neuhaus and I wrote our little book *To Empower People*, in which we urged a rethinking of social policy in this country in terms of mediating structures; this same idea animated the Mediating Structures Project of the American Enterprise Institute, which between 1976 and 1979 explored the applicability of this concept to specific policy areas. I would like to stress that we are not suggesting a panacea or magic formula here; this is a flexible, empirically testable concept. And much of the testing remains to be done.

Mediating structures are so important for a new model of the welfare state because the *old* model so fatally ignores them. The European model of the welfare state, which continues to inspire American liberals, is strictly dualistic: On one side is the state, as the supplier of social services; on the other side are individuals, with their rights and entitlements; *there is nothing in between*. Or, if there is, it is perceived as an obstacle. It is precisely this sociological blindness that has led to the welfare state as a centralized, bureaucratized, professionalized monopoly, which more and more of its intended beneficiaries perceive as an alien imposition. We don't have to disparage the old model unduly (most of us, I'm sure, would rather live in western Europe—if pressed, I'd even include Sweden—than in most other countries of the world); there is a lot of institutionalized concern and decency there; *but I think that we can do better!*

Before the coming of the modern welfare state, of course, *all* social services were provided by these institutions. As I have said before, it cannot be our purpose to return to that situation. However, neither must we stand by helplessly as the welfare state gobbles up or cripples these institutions one by one. An important feature of the new model can be stated in the old phrasing of the Hippocratic Oath: "Do no harm!"—in this case, no harm to mediating structures. The state should not needlessly duplicate what mediating structures are doing: This means cognizance of all the private initiatives in play, and the planning of state actions *around*, and not against, them. Also it means that the state should not inhibit these private initiatives by foolish and unnecessary regulation—this implies a massive effort of what Robert Woodson once called *social deregulation*. These policies are, if you will, negative in the sense of letting mediating structures do their thing; their effects would be very positive indeed. There is an impressive agenda here for policy revamping and for legislation.

Then there is an equally impressive agenda of positive support for mediating structures. This can be done through a variety of mechanisms, the details of which, I'm sure, will have to vary as between different policy areas—*direct subsidies or grants, tax incentives* (mostly relevant to business as a possible supplier of social services), *tax credits*. I do not minimize the problems with some of these mechanisms (especially the problem of creating wondrous new pork-barrels) but I'm convinced that these problems can be solved. In terms of mechanisms, I think that the *voucher concept* will increasingly be turned to as the new model is being constructed. If you go over the aforementioned criteria, I think you will find that each one suggests a voucher mechanism. And most people, if given a choice, will "cash in" their vouchers at this or that mediating structure, either already in existence or newly set up to provide a particular service.

I'm sure you realize by now that I could go on and on about this. Let me instead ask the question that Lenin asked on the eve of the Russian Revolution: *"What is to be done?"* Well, let there be no doubt about it. To bring about such a new model of the welfare state in its fullblown shape would require nothing less than a social revolution! What is more, this revolution would have to be fought in the political arena against very powerful and well-organized vested interests—all those who profit from the present system. Perhaps you can envisage such a revolution as a politically realistic project. Both as a conservative and as a sociologist, I'm skeptical. (As a conservative, I prefer gradual change to revolutions as a matter of principle; as a sociologist, I know that most revolutions have high and unanticipated costs.) What, then, *is* to be done?

It seems to me that, first, those of us who think along these lines should actually produce *an alternative vision of the welfare state*, in as much detail as we can manage to put in. Let us draw a picture: Look, this is what this thing would look like—even if we can't get there right away. Closely related to this, we should start using a *new language* to talk about social policy—a new rhetoric, if you will—to break the absurd monopoly that liberalism has enjoyed in this area. And then we should think, in politically realistic ways, of the *immediate (and necessarily smaller) steps* that would take us closer to the model. This means very concrete policy designs and legislative proposals. A very first step would be to undertake a comprehensive survey of social programs (at least on the federal level) that impinge on mediating structures—and to start thinking of mediating-structures-oriented alternatives. There is enough business here to keep a lot of people out of mischief for quite a long time!

Let me conclude by making some observations about the political context of all this, both domestically and internationally. The crisis of the welfare state is common now to all Western-style democracies. But the United States, I believe, has a unique opportunity to take the lead in finding a way out of the crisis. The reason for this is, quite simply, that mediating structures are stronger in America than in other countries. American pluralism and the American tradition of voluntary association continue to be vital societal resources. Just for this reason it is quite absurd that so many people continue to be fixated on the European model. At the same time, it is very likely that, if America takes the lead, other democracies will take note and quite possibly emulate whatever is applicable to their own problems.

Within the domestic political situation, most of what I have said here is not readily recognizable as being either conservative or liberal, right or left of center. Especially the mediating structures concept cuts across the ideological divides. Thus, in theory, the concept could be picked up by either Republicans or Democrats. The latter scenario, though, is less probable, and for a very simple reason: The Democratic party, as it is now constituted, is much more captive to the vested interests that would preserve the *status quo* in social policy. Also, the intellectuals feeding ideas to the Democratic party are just the ones who are fixated on the old, European-style model of the welfare state. It seems to me that, politically speaking, what we have here is a *great Republican opportunity.* (I want to stress that I say this as a sociologist. True, I'm a registered Republican—in my milieu in Boston this is almost as piquant as being a certified lunatic or a convicted bigamist— and I would like the Republican party to make use of its opportunities. But I'm pretty sure that I would make the same socio-political diagnosis if I were on the other side of the fence.)

A final comment on the international context: For many years now my main interest as a sociologist has been on modernization processes in the Third World, and accordingly I have been more concerned with questions of U.S. foreign policy than with domestic policy issues. In this context I find it ludicrous that the United States is so widely perceived as a power blindly committed to the *status quo.* In actual fact, socially and culturally, American society is the most innovative and dynamic in the world. One could even say that the American revolution is the only *real* revolution going on; the other so-called revolutions are, most of them, reactionary projects pushing people back into age-old structures of oppression, stagnation, and misery. It seems to me high time that America turn its innovative genius to a re-structuring of social policy. We are in the position of creating a new vision of a humane society superior to anything existing today and of making people everywhere take note of this vision. Such a turn, besides its domestic benefits, would also have a far from inconsiderable impact on the international image of this country.